Parent Partnership in the Early Years

Other Classmates:

2nd Series

Successful Subject Co-ordination – Christine Farmery
Playing Outdoors in the Early Years – Ros Garrick
Assemblies Made Easy – Victoria Kidwell
Homework – Victoria Kidwell
Getting Promoted – Tom Miller
ICT in the Early Years – Mark O'Hara
Creating Positive Classrooms – Mike Ollerton
Getting Organized – Angela Thody and
Derek Bowden
Physical Development in the Early Years –
Lynda Woodfield

1st Series

Lesson Planning – Graham Butt
Managing Your Classroom – Gererd Dixie
Teacher's Guide to Protecting Children – Janet Kay
Tips for Trips – Andy Leeder
Stress Busting – Michael Papworth
Every Minute Counts – Michael Papworth
Teaching Poetry – Fred Sedgwick
Running Your Tutor Group – Ian Startup
Involving Parents – Julian Stern
Marking and Assessment – Howard Tanner

Parent Partnership in the Early Years

Damien Fitzgerald

continuum
LONDON • NEW YORK

Continuum

The Tower Building
11 York Road
London SE1 7NX

15 East 26th Street
New York
NY 10010

British Library Cataloguing-in-Publication Data
A catalogue record for this book is available from the British Library.

ISBN 0–8264–6873–X (paperback)

Typeset by BookEns Ltd, Royston, Herts.
Printed and bound in Great Britain by
Antony Rowe Ltd, Chippenham, Wiltshire

Contents

Contents

Introduction

Partnerships within early years settings are about reciprocal relationships: the influence that the family has on the setting and the influence of the setting on the family. They are also about relationships with the wider community. The Curriculum Guidance (QCA/ DfEE, 2000), the key guidance document for early years education in England, states that parents are central partners in their child's education and practitioners need to work effectively with them. Working in partnership with parents within early years settings requires discussion and consultation. It may also require planning and action between the setting, other organizations and stakeholders. This may include practitioners from different agencies, government bodies, the voluntary sector and local authorities (National Children's Bureau, 2000). Although of great value, this shows that to achieve effective parental partnerships requires a range of skills and qualities, a commitment to sharing of information, and shared goals in terms of outcome. In this book the term 'parent' is used to describe all those who take on the role of parent (Daper and Duffy, 2001), irrespective of biological status, culture or gender.

In the 1940s schools were generally seen as an extension of the community and staff tended to live within the communities they worked in (Adams and Christenson, 2000). This made social contact as well as professional interaction more likely. Today, family and community structures make this pattern less likely. For example, many practitioners live outside the community they work in and have less participation within it. Alongside this many initiatives in early education and care have been implemented. The result of this is that establishing and maintaining effective parental partnerships is a challenge for practitioners.

It takes commitment, time and a range of skills for early years settings to establish effective partnerships. This book explores how different issues have influenced partnership working and shows that even though achieving partnerships can be demanding there are significant benefits to be gained for families and the setting. From this a number of practitioner skills are discussed that can contribute to the development and maintenance of effective partnerships. A range of practical approaches are identified to assist early years practitioners in working collaboratively with parents, including issues specific to fathers. Alongside this it is important to acknowledge that barriers to partnership can occur, but approaches for practitioners to identify and resolve these are suggested.

Any development in practice self-evaluation can provide valuable information about benefits and future directions. The final section of the book explores approaches to guide self-evaluation during and following changes to practice.

1

The Move Towards Parental Partnerships

Historical influences

From the early twentieth century Margaret McMillan was a central pioneer in the development of early education. She was among the first to state that parental involvement, which predominantly focused on the mother but did recognize the role of fathers, was important (Steedman, 1990). Even though this was a positive step towards parental involvement many obstacles to developing partnerships with parents followed.

During the period 1920–30 the involvement of practitioners with families was rooted in the 'compensatory model'. This emphasized the importance of practitioner involvement in children's education as the home environment or parenting was seen as having deficits in areas that were important for child development. This was demonstrated in 1931 by the Hadow report. It noted the benefits of teachers talking to parents about health and hygiene, but this was based on the premiss that families were seen as lacking knowledge to deal proficiently with these issues themselves.

Smidt (2002) describes the role that was often

attributed to parents over the next decades: good parents helped children by supporting what happened in nursery or school; bad parents held children back leading to supposed deficits. Many past intervention programmes emphasized the role of schools and teachers in educating these parents about the impact it was having on their children. Edwards and Warin (1999) explain this clearly. Home was expected to create a willing pupil, ready and able to receive knowledge, but this reduces the parental role to acting as the 'teacher's agent'. These approaches were well-intentioned, but the relationship between home and school involved no elements of partnership. The deciding factor in the good–bad parent debate was based entirely on the parent offering their support to enable educational establishments to achieve their agenda and taking little or no account of the needs and views of the family.

In Britain it was not until 1967 that the first clear recognition of the contribution of parents to their child's learning emerged. The Plowden report stated:

One of the essentials for educational advance is a closer partnership between the two parties (i.e. schools and parents) to every child's education. (Plowden, 1967, p. 37)

Following Plowden, the importance of partnership, based on equal representation (Lawson, 2003), became recognized. However this was potentially a position that did not provide the basis for effective partnership working. In many respects, additional stimulation and education was still often deemed as necessary to compensate for the poverty and social disadvantage experienced by children in deprived areas. Long (2000) demonstrates this clearly in a recent publication that refers to negative impact often associated with class status and poverty levels in families:

It seems likely then, that although educational disadvantage is closely related to family class and poverty, it is still possible to compensate for this to a significant extent (p. 170)

This approach emphasizes the role of practitioners in supporting the development of children by providing a suitable early education environment, but it is not conducive to establishing effective and respectful partnerships. In particular, the cultural background of families and communities and the role of parents in promoting children's early development was not fully recognized (Bruce and Meggitt, 2002).

During the late 1990s there were many initiatives in early years education, such as nursery vouchers (now abandoned), expansion of childcare places through the National Childcare Strategy, and the childcare element of Working Tax Credit. Many of these have led to parents being seen as consumers of early years education and care. But even though this approach avoids labelling families as having deficits, it does not necessarily recognize the importance of reciprocal relationships, a vital element for partnership working (Curtis, 1998; Epstein and Saunders, 2002).

Edwards and Knight (1997) argue that a consumer view of education reduces teaching to a technical operation rather than a complex profession and this is inappropriate for describing the educational experiences of young children. The development of close partnerships, with shared aims, can help to prevent the emergence of this concept. Although Foot *et al.* (2000) believe that the view of parents as consumers has given way to recognition of parents as partners, they suggest that practitioners and parents may feel unease at the empowerment this can bring for various reasons. For example, parents may feel they lack skills and practitioners can be over-challenged by the expectations to develop trusting relationships with all parents.

A clear example of the move towards seeing parents as partners is provided in *The Curriculum Guidance for the Foundation Stage* in England, which was published in 2000:

When parents and practitioners work together in early years settings, the results have appositive impact on the child's development and learning. Therefore, each setting should seek to develop an effective partnership with parents (QCA/DfEE, 2000, p. 9)

The guidance also recognizes that, although early years settings make an important contribution to learning, the home environment and family contribution are of prime importance because 'parents continue to have a prime teaching role with their children' (*op. cit.*, 22). So although the move towards seeing parents as equal partners in the relationship has been slow, the foundations for further developments through national policies are now clearly in place.

2

Partnership with Parents

The development of parental partnerships

Although practice has progressed over recent decades, some practitioners continue to see parents as problematic. It also has to be acknowledged that some parents do not want the closeness of the relationship advocated by the emphasis on parental involvement (Curtis, 1998).

To establish partnerships with families connections need to be made, information exchanged and links developed in a way that values and respects the contributions of the children, their family and the setting. To realize the benefits of shared working, parents and practitioners need to have a shared sense of what is meant by the term partnership (Lawson, 2003), which emphasizes the process of information sharing and communication. A common understanding is vital and it cannot be assumed that all stakeholders share the same view. Keyes (2002) highlights this by presenting two perspectives on the relationship between home and school. One sees an effective separation of roles and functions between home and school, but with each having a mutual respect for the other as illustrated in Story A. In the other, as illustrated in Story B, the setting functions as an extended family, with a clear link between the home and setting.

Story A

Greenacre Primary School is a small school situated on the outskirts of a town. There are 26 children in the nursery, which is staffed by two full-time and one part-time practitioner. Children are admitted at two points during the year, following their third birthday. Parents of children are invited to a one-hour introductory meeting two weeks prior to their starting at nursery. The routines of the nursery are explained. Opportunities are given for parents to ask questions within the group. Children generally stay with their parent in the school hall.

Story B

Following a home visit parents are sent a pack of information prior to their child starting at the setting. They are encouraged to visit the setting with their child to see if they feel it is suitable. At this initial visit parents and children are introduced to the practitioner who will be their key worker if the child attends the setting. Information is exchanged and there are opportunities for families and practitioners to ask questions. Each parent is given opportunities to ask questions and, if necessary, a time is agreed to talk with the key worker again about any specific issues.

In Story B, connections are made and the beginning of a successful partnership is developed. This initial start is an important part of children developing a positive approach to learning from home, the early years setting and the community (Epstein and Saunders, 2002).

What are the benefits of family partnership?

Daper and Duffy (2001) raise two questions in relation to parental partnership: why aim for increased levels of partnership working and what are the challenges? The knowledge that each party brings to the partnership has unique elements. Families know about the home situation, their extended family, important people, culture, history, health, adversities and issues related to the individual child. Practitioners know about the needs of all children in the setting, child development, learning, curriculum activities and peer relationships (Keyser, 2001).

Story A

Jane's parents arrive at nursery on her first day not quite sure what to expect. Some of their questions were answered at the introductory session but they still feel unsure and Jane is nervous. During the first session some of the practitioners explain parts of the routine and make reference to what parents need *to do*. There is a brief opportunity to talk at the end of the session before they all leave, but a comment is made about Jane *'being fine tomorrow on her own'*. From this it is clear that the nursery presumes Jane's parents will not stay.

Story B

Tariq is looking forward to going to nursery because he will see Sarah and Tom, two of the practitioners that he met during a home visit. His parents also found the information pack from the nursery useful, as the family have been able to talk about different aspects of nursery. During the first session Tariq's parents are encouraged to play alongside him. His key worker suggests that during the first week it is good to have someone around as this will help Tariq to settle and will help to build links between nursery and home. After a few days, when Tariq is playing happily with a new friend, Tom suggests they leave him for about twenty minutes and join a parents' group in the school community room.

In Story B there are many opportunities for the exchange of information. This is likely to lead to a smoother transition and practitioners and parents having a shared understanding of how the home and setting contribute to each child's development. Bruce (1997) describes this approach as interactionist, where the sharing of information and knowledge between parents and practitioners leads to mutual benefits. Early acknowledgement of these different, but unique, perspectives will help to empower parents by showing that the different contributions are important in supporting the development of children and practitioners.

Effective partnerships contribute to parents having a more positive attitude towards the setting. Additionally, children are likely to see less of a divide between home and nursery when their family are valued by the practitioners. For parents, benefits include increased levels of self-confidence, a wider understanding of the aims of the educational setting and the curriculum, and awareness of the opportunities of the home as a learning environment (Eldridge, 2001). Sure Start (2000) highlight the importance of establishing continuity between home and the setting to develop relationships and empower parents. This greater level of involvement can also produce benefits for practitioners by enhancing understanding of the family culture, lead to deeper respect for the family (a central requirement for partnership development) and increased satisfaction with the quality of their practice.

A number of studies have investigated the benefits for children when their parents have formed partnerships with the setting. These have identified clear correlations with increased achievement, better attendance, an improved attitude to learning and less behaviour problems. Parents with higher levels of involvement also devote more time to assisting children at home and this is likely to be beneficial in terms of development and learning (Caplan *et al.*, 1997; Curtis, 1998; Chaboudy *et al.*, 2001). For children, the importance of a smooth transition into the early years setting is vital, as shown in the case studies. For parents, the likelihood of them taking a significant role will be influenced by the ethos of the setting and the qualities displayed by practitioners (see Story A and B below).

Story A (one year after starting)

Jane has been attending the school nursery for one year. During this time she has had settled periods at nursery but these have been erratic and her attendance has been poor. Dad usually brings Jane to nursery and her mum collects her. Although the relationship between her parents and practitioners is respectful, they rarely chat about her day or other issues. Jane's key worker wants to involve her parents more but feels as though she has not been able to find the right opportunity.

Story B (one year after starting)

A year after starting Tariq has had good attendance at nursery and seems to be very happy. On most days he will take something home from nursery and his parents often comment about how this forms part of his learning experiences at home. During the year issues have arisen, but the positive relationship developed between Tariq's parents and key worker has meant these have been dealt with. Most weeks, Tariq's mum or dad try to come into nursery and spend short periods reading to interested children, individually and in small groups.

The benefits of creating positive relationships to be built on during the early years of education cannot be over emphasized. The earlier that partnership with each family can be established, the longer it is likely to be sustained throughout the child's education and the more significant the gain (Eldridge, 2001).

The role of practitioners in developing effective partnerships

A number of qualities have been cited as contributing to the establishment and maintenance of effective partnerships. McWilliam *et al.* (1998) summarize important qualities as family orientation, positiveness, sensitivity, responsiveness and friendliness. They state that services based on these qualities lead to an open door along what is described as the *path of family orientation*, as shown in Figure 1. Although the qualities are of equal importance they stress that it is still necessary for each to be present to open the door to family access and empowerment. Alongside these, they also argue that services need to possess child and community skills. This covers areas such as knowledge of child development and interacting with children and awareness of issues within the community.

Positiveness, sensitivity, responsiveness and friendliness can all be demonstrated through effective communication and form a central element of establishing and maintaining effective partnerships. To respond to the needs of families within the community, communication needs to be sensitive in terms of culture, social status and lifestyle. Effective communication is a powerful factor in facilitating quality parental involvement (Jordan *et al.*, 1998; Keyes, 2002).

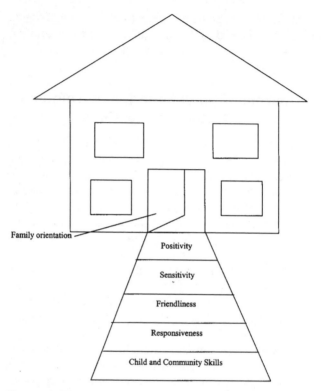

Figure 1: The path to the family orientation door

Within effective partnerships parents and practitioners have identified trust as a vital element (Bruce and Meggitt, 2002; Dalli, 2002). Adams and Christenson (2000) define trust as:

Confidence that another person will act in a way to benefit or sustain the relationship, or the implicit or explicit goals of the relationship, to achieve positive outcome for students (p. 480)

This is important as it recognizes the range of interfaces necessary for the development of a trusting partnership: the need to sustain a strong connection between the partners; the need to address the ongoing needs of children; and the need for continued effort to sustain it. Evidence for this is provided in the finding that the lower the level of trust in relationships the less likely either partner is to recognize the other's positive attributes.

The qualities described by McWilliam *et al.* (1998) (see Figure 1) are promoted in partnerships built on mutual respect. Although greater levels of parental partnership bring benefits to children, families and educational settings; it can also increase the focus on parenting. It is impotent for practitioners to be aware of this, as Braun (2001) states this can lead to parents questioning their abilities. To support parents effectively, and avoid this becoming a negative factor in relationships, practitioners need to show acceptance for the choices each parent and family make in how to carry out their parenting role. Within partnerships it is likely that differences will arise and, although consensus may not be reached, it is important to have respect for different views and the choices that families make (Curtis, 1998; Whalley, 2001; Moyles *et al.*, 2002; Smidt, 2002). A consequence of this may be that a particular issue or challenge is not fully resolved, but by respecting the choice that is made the situation can be dealt with in a more amicable manner, which is likely to leave an *open door* for dealing with future issues cooperatively, as shown in the story below. This can be particularly important in early years settings, as many parents are relatively new to the environment.

Story

Jo enjoys playing outside but on the past two days has fallen and grazed her arm and leg whilst playing on the slide. Her mum is upset by this and tells Jo's key worker that if equipment is not safe it should be removed. Tom listens attentively to Jo's mum's concerns and thanks her for taking the time to come and talk it over. He explains that many children, including Jo, have been playing on the slide happily for several weeks and that time to explore and develop physical skills outside is important. Nevertheless, Tom suggests that over the next few days he or another practitioner will spend some time with the children using the slide to see if there is anything that needs to be improved. Finally, he arranges a time at the end of the week to meet with Jo's mum again where they can review the situation. Although not what she initially wanted, Jo's mum feels that her concerns have been listened to and can see that there are benefits to outside provision.

Within parent–practitioner partnerships issues of balance of power arise, with power often implicitly resting with practitioners. This is because as the service provider they offer the services that families want access to, and because interactions generally take place within the early years setting–practitioner territory. Moves towards partnership though can involve blurring of traditional roles between practitioners and parents (Edwards and Knight, 1997). There can be many benefits from this, but it can also be a potential source of conflict as practitioners, much the same as parents, may question their abilities. The changes associated with moving towards a position where parents are seen as partners, rather than clients, is shown in Figure 2.

This continuum can provide a useful guide for early years settings to evaluate where they currently are and decide in what areas they can increase partnership with parents. Foot *et al.*, (2000) explain how there is a link between parent and staff participation and the quality of provision. Support for this also comes from recent findings from the Effective Provision of Pre-School Education (EPPE) project, which emphasizes the importance of home learning and the proactive stance that practitioners could take to support this (Sylva *et al.*, 2003).

To help equalize the power base between practitioners and parents Whalley (2001) argues that creating an environment where parents are encouraged to question, challenge and make choices suitable to their needs is vital. This also shows a commitment to using communication to establish equal partnership and ensure each party has influence (Greenman, 2001; Keyser, 2001). The benefits of this were an increased willingness among parents to share understanding of their children's learning at home, which recognizes the role of parents as their child's primary educator (QCA/DfEE,

Parent on the premises

| Parents as clients | Use a room for their own purpose | Attends school, e.g. parent conference | Regularly help, but with mundane tasks | Take a regular role in supervising activities | Lead activities, e.g. working with a small group, gardening | Reinforces learning started by practitioners | Parents as partners |

Parent off the premises

| Attends school, e.g. fun day | Helps with activities at home, e.g. making resources | Help with school trips |

Figure 2: Partnership Continuum

Adapted from Edwards, A. and Knight, P. (1997) 'Parents and Professionals'. In B. Cosin and M. Hales (eds) *Families, Education and Social Differences*, London: Routledge (p. 71)

2000). In contrast, it has been argued that equality is not a vital factor in partnership as long as there is recognition of the different perspectives and power that each partner has. To take this a step further, the partner most likely to have a greater stake in the relationship is the parent, as their investment will last longer than any individual practitioner (Todd and Higgins, 1998) and recognition of this is likely to support partnership working.

An additional factor in determining the successfulness of partnership is the qualities and enthusiasm brought to the process by practitioners. Practitioners who display warmth, openness, sensitivity, flexibility, reliability and accessibility to parents have a positive impact on family–practitioner partnerships (Keyes, 2002). Thinking back to the last story, Tom provides a good model of this in action. To demonstrate these qualities practitioners do not have to go to special lengths or make significant alterations to their practice. Small gestures, such as being prepared to listen attentively, showing genuine interest in a situation and being prepared to respond to a particular need, can have significant benefits in building relationships (Hall *et al.*, 2001). When asked, parents identify a number of factors they feel are important in practitioners. These include: being able to access practitioners to discuss concerns, offering feedback on child performance, a positive attitude to parents and willingness to deal with complaints (Foot *et al.*, 2000), which confirms the importance of simple actions that make practitioners accessible. Perhaps the central message in forming partnerships is the recognition that there is a commonality between parents and practitioners, with each portraying passion, care and commitment to the welfare of children (Lawson, 2003).

A challenge for practitioners is to find consensus in the approach that is likely to achieve the best outcome for children, families and early years settings. To develop this, practitioners need to think in terms of developing current practices to gain even more benefits, rather than from the perspective of improving a poor situation. Dahlberg *et al.* (1999) capture the challenges and opportunities presented for early years settings in establishing effective partnerships with families and communities, by talking of the:

Need to promote an informed participatory and critical local democracy – early childhood institutions have the potential to be places where parents, politicians and others can come together with pedagogues and children to engage in dialogue on a range of subjects (p. 77)

Communication

Effective communication between practitioners and families is essential to developing partnerships (Anderson *et al.*, 2002). The United States Department of Education (2002) highlights the importance of communication in terms of the information it can give parents in helping them to understand the aims of early education; awareness of how their child's learning is progressing; and how to help children at home. The message from families is that they want to be communicated with, kept informed and have information shared with them (Adams and Chistenson, 2000). For partnerships to be maintained, it is vital that there are effective strategies in place to facilitate two-directional communication and support. This is especially critical in early years environments, as for many families it is likely to be their first contact with education and care settings.

In many ways the challenge of establishing and maintaining effective communication has increased due to the expansion of early years provision. Initiatives such as the introduction of different types of provision, the creation of new provision (e.g. Sure Start) and multi-agency working have expanded greatly (Pugh, 2001). The important basis remains unchanged: the need to ensure two-way communication where both parties contribute. The need to maintain positive interactions is also important for children as they can associate negative interactions with their behaviour, especially if there is poor communication between the home and setting (Lawson, 2003), as was shown earlier in the story of Jane. For example, if there is disagreement between a parent and practitioner, and this remains unresolved, a child may believe that this has occurred because they have behaved poorly or done something wrong. To maximize family partnership opportunities, communication should have the following properties:

- two-directional (with opportunities for each party to respond appropriately);

- take place formally and informally;

- offer feedback to families about their children's progress;

- find out the families' opinions about the early years setting;

- involve families in decision-making processes.

(National Centre for Early Development and Learning, 1999; Eldridge, 2001).

To meet these expectations it can be useful to plan in advance how contacts will be made with each individual family. An example of this is provided in Figure 3, which outlines a planned programme for formal and informal communication. For practitioners this may involve a fundamental, but worthwhile change to communication that Malaguzzi (1998) describes:

Teachers must leave behind an isolated silent mode of working that leaves no traces. Instead they must discover ways to communicate and document the children's evolving experiences at school. They must prepare a steady flow of quality information targeted to parents but appreciated also by children and teachers. (p. 69–70)

Models of partnership

A number of different models have been used to describe the form that partnerships can take. Although it is unlikely that practice in a particular setting will exactly reflect one model, they can potentially provide a starting point for practitioners to reflect how current practice and procedures compare and consider what developments they want to implement to enhance partnership with families. Epstein and Saunders (2002) describe a continuum of partnership models:

	Type of communication	
Autumn	Home visit. Parent meeting or conference (may focus on how the child is settling and take place informally).	Telephone call to give an opportunity to exchange information.
Spring	Parent meeting or conference (may focus on areas of learning, progress and opportunities for shared learning).	Informal contact (e.g. a note to home or discussion over coffee with some parents and a key worker) to share information about the child's progress.
Summer	Telephone call or informal meeting in the setting to maintain contact and provide an opportunity to raise any issues (e.g. transition to a new setting).	Written report to provide a summary of the progress the child has made during the year.

Figure 3: Communication: Outline timetable

- **Protective model** – this operates along the lines of a business and requires parents to delegate responsibility for education to the setting as the aims of home and the setting and the roles of practitioners and parents are different.

- **School-to-home transmission model** – this model recognizes the importance of the family but only places an emphasis on one directional communication – from the setting to the home and assumes a level of parental agreement with decisions taken by the setting. In this model there is likely to be little sharing of ideas between the setting and community.

- **Curriculum enrichment model** – this model recognizes the benefits of collaborative learning between practitioners, parents and children and integrates knowledge from families and the community into the curriculum and learning. There is a focus on the curriculum as this is seen as an important vehicle for impacting on learning.

- **Partnership model** – this model is built on long-term commitment, mutual respect and wide-spread involvement of families and practitioners at different levels, such as joint planning and shared decision-making. It reflects the fact the children are embedded in and influenced by the home, the setting and the community.

Epstein and Saunders (2002) also identify six descriptors of parental involvement: parenting; communicating; volunteering; learning at home; decision-making and collaborating. At a parenting level, schools provide information to families and the setting listens to information from the home to learn about the needs of the child. The volunteering style recognizes and utilizes the support family members and the community can offer to enhance the curriculum. The learning-at-home style of involvement is based around curriculum enhancement but aims to provide guidance to parents about strategies for extending children's understanding and awareness of the curriculum. The highest level of parental involvement, collaborating with the community, is about both utilizing and contributing to provision and service provision within the community. This can have benefits in terms of assisting families to access community services and in establishing links between the community and early years settings. An outline of how these issues may impact on practice is given in Figure 4, which shows the role that parents and practitioners may take and how this could be understood and interpreted by the child.

Although use of descriptions such as these may have limitations it does alert practitioners to the need to see partnership from two perspectives: the practices and provision of the setting and the choices that parents make. It is important to accept and understand that each family will be able to commit to different levels of involvement. If the level of involvement from some families is low it can be frustrating, but respecting this and aiming to offer support is far more likely to ensure that families remain involved, and over time they may be able to offer increased levels of involvement.

Model of partnership	The role of parents	The role of practitioners	The experience of children
Protective	Assume little responsibility in education. Involvement is very limited, e.g. collecting children and attending special events.	See themselves as the primary educators of children.	Will see little interaction between home and the setting. May experience difficulties with setting and begin to dislike coming.
School to home	Parents agree with decisions made by the setting and respond to information or requests from the setting.	Involve the family in some aspects of education, e.g. asking parents to read to their child. Rarely ask the opinion of parents.	Will see some communication between home and parents. Some aspects of learning will be continued at home.
Curriculum Enrichment	Will be encouraged to take an active role in the setting and contribute where possible. Parents will be involved in various aspects of the curriculum.	Include experiences from parents and the community in the curriculum, e.g. invite speakers, organize visits to parts of the community and encourage children to talk about events important to them.	Experiences from home and the community will be part of learning. Will see parents taking a role in learning at home and in the setting.
Partnership	Take a full role in the setting and contribute to decisions about learning and development. Parents feel involved, respected and see themselves as central to the learning process.	Utilize all opportunities for communication with and involving parents. Work cooperatively with parents to ensure that learning experiences of children are influenced by home.	Coordinated learning between the home and setting. Evidence of family in the setting, e.g. family book, parents helping. Will see positive communication between parents and practitioners, which is likely to enhance feelings of security.

Figure 4: Models of partnership

3

Strategies for Working with Families

The discussion of what partnership is and the ways practitioners can promote it are borne out in practice with families, both within and outside educational settings. Contact with families in settings takes place in different contexts, from informal chat and information exchange at the beginning or end of a session, to more formal contact, perhaps through parent conferences or a set of planned workshops (Smidt, 2002). The overriding issue to guide work with families is about establishing effective partnerships that allow for an exchange of information. To do this, settings need to work well with parents as well as children. To achieve this, settings need to reach out to families, which includes recognizing differences, valuing diversity and accepting the choices parents make about involvement (Epstein and Saunders, 2002). This section details a range of strategies for promoting partnership with families and offers practical examples from literature and practitioners.

Policies and procedures

An important factor in determining the quality of parental involvement is the extent to which family partnership forms a central part of the setting's philosophy and practices (Bailey, 2001; Eldridge, 2001). Questions need to be asked about the level of partnership with families. Do all team members share the family focus? Were families involved in constructing the philosophy of the setting? Does practice recognize, respond and include the diverse needs of all members of the community? Are the philosophies and statements in policies evident in practice? Bailey (2001) describes three themes around family involvement and support that can guide policy formation and practice:

♦ parent involvement needs to be individualized and reflect the diversity of families;

♦ parents need to be active partners and be given opportunities to participate;

♦ services should be organized in ways that allow and enable families to feel competent.

Although this shows that policies reaffirming family partnership are not enough on their own, they have a place in formulating and guiding high quality practice. A family handbook can be used to emphasize the elements of policy on working in partnership with families that the setting promotes; the steps that are taken to ensure all families are welcome, valued and respected; and that two-way communication is at the heart of the setting's philosophy (Keyser, 2001).

Home visits

From the family perspective it was found that parents valued visits that take place prior to the child starting at a new setting (Jordan *et al.,* 1998, Roggman *et al.,* 2001). Home visits can provide an opportunity to identify concerns and pass on information, both to and from parents. Even though home visits can be a useful in supporting transition into the early years setting, a family may choose not to be visited and this decision needs to be respected (Smidt, 2002).

The successfulness of visits is clearly related to the strategies used and promotion of parental engagement. A systematic recording format, as shown in Figure 5, will be useful in ensuring coverage of relevant areas and to provide an outline structure for the visit.

Bruce and Meggitt (2002) suggest it can be useful to involve two practitioners when planning home visits. One is able to play and interact with the child and the other listen attentively to the parent(s). The benefits of this approach are described in Figure 6.

Transitions into early years settings

Transition into an early years environment for the first time can be very challenging for families. Children are likely to find transitions easier and enjoy exploration more fully when they feel that their attachment to their parents (who are likely to have been the primary care providers up to this point) is not threatened (Ainsworth *et al.,* 1978). Prior to starting at the setting, information gathered at past meetings (e.g. home visits) will provide a valuable insight into strategies and comforting routines for supporting the child.

Name:	Address
Date of birth:	

Family/friend contact details		
Contact 1	Contact 2	Contact 3

Doctor Contact details	Medical details/allergies

Professional/multi-agency contact details	
Name and organization details	Notes

Figure 5: Example of a home visit information form

Thoughts on school	Pre-school experiences

Interests	Comforters

Worries or concerns about school

Details of additional adults who can collect	

Figure 5, cont.

Parent Partnership in the Early Years

I work in a reception class with support from a full-time nursery nurse. The children start school at different times of the year according to their age, the three intakes being September, October and January. They will have attended different nurseries and preschools and in some cases the children will not know anyone within their new reception class until the day they start school. This would also apply to the adults who will be looking after them if we did not undertake home visits a few weeks or days before they are due to start school.

Home visits were established by the Head teacher and have had a positive influence on the reception children, parents and teachers for many years. There are many reasons for the visit, the main one being, an opportunity for the child to meet the class teacher and nursery nurse and vice versa. These informal visits last for about 30 minutes and involve the nursery nurse and myself going to the child's home. There we will talk to a parent or parents and play with the child. Over the years we have found that the parents enjoy chatting to the nursery nurse. They ask questions about simple school routine for example, where will I meet my child after the school day? How much do school meals cost? Just gaining answers to simple worries and getting to know the nursery nurse helps them to become more at ease with what will happen and who will take care of their child once they say goodbye to them.

The children enjoy home visits as it gives them a chance to meet us in their environment. We take jigsaws, books and games from school and my role during the visit is usually on the floor playing and talking with the child. Sometimes parents can feel that we are assessing their child, but we reassure them that it is simply (but importantly) an opportunity for us to get an idea of what the child enjoys doing, what they are looking forward to about school and what they may be worried about.

Parents raise their children instilling the importance of `stranger danger'. Yet they take them to school and in some cases leave them with strangers. Home visits enable the children to see that their new teachers are invited into their home and are accepted by their parents as people who can be trusted.

All these points add up to a more confident child entering a reception class on their first daunting day at school, and parents who feel less anxious having talked through their concerns and recognized that their children will be in safe, caring hands. The benefits of two people undertaking the home visit is that parents have someone in the classroom who they have met and can talk to at the beginning or end of the day, which is invaluable in building a trusting relationship.

Altogether, the settling-in period is a much happier time where children can concentrate on getting to know each other, making new friends and having fun in a learning environment.

Figure 6: A practitioner account of successful home visits

Part of the practitioner's role prior to and during transition is providing reassurance to parents that their child will cope with the change and promoting family participation in the transition plan (Kraft-Sayre and Pianta, 2000). This can be offered by stressing the cognitive competencies of the child and reference to the new opportunities the setting will provide to complement the learning experiences at home. Through regular contact, the key worker and family will become familiar with each other and a trusting relationship is likely to form. This is important, as the higher the level of agreement about the child between the practitioner and parent, the more optimistic the parent is likely to be about the transition (Griebel and Niesel, 2002). To develop trust with parents and show awareness and respect for different family structures, Neuman (2002) stresses that procedures and working practices that support these principles need to be in place. This includes use of documentation that avoids stereotypic language, support for parents who have English as an additional language, and information about inclusion of children with special educational needs.

In Sweden, transition periods can last for up to two weeks and parents spend significant amounts of time with their children in the setting. For many parents, working commitments could make this difficult, but perhaps there is a role here for settings, after gaining parental permission, to contact the workplace of each parent and provide them with information about the transition process and ask for their support. Finland makes use of child portfolios for explaining the routines and aims of the setting and recording early experiences of life at the setting for the child and parent (Neuman, 2002). As well as providing important information this also sets the basis for early development of the partnership approach and continued parental involvement. To ensure high attendance, and provide a rewarding experience for all parties at transition visits, it can be useful to limit the number of parents attending at once by sending personal invitations to families (Smidt, 2002).

Drawing these points together, Dalli (2002) summarizes a number of strategies that can support the transitions process, including:

- providing families with printed and oral informa- tion about the setting, routines and settling-in procedure prior to the child starting;

- having a specific practitioner to communicate with about transition;

- respecting and responding to input from parents about how to support their child during transition;

- practitioners should proactively approach children during transition periods to support them and assist in the 'fitting-in' process;

- practitioners need to be aware of strategies to ease anxieties that parents may be feeling and use these to offer support.

Parent conferences

Meetings with parents to discuss the progress that their child is making provide valuable opportunities for two-way communication. Due to time constraints they are often rushed and can consist of practitioners passing on information. This leaves little room for discussion or debate and makes the communication one-directional and less effective. To ensure that parental meetings are based on two-directional communication, more in the style of a conference, practitioners can use documentation, photographic evidence, anecdotal notes and examples of children's work to make it more interactive. Parents can be asked to contribute some of the evidence. This will encourage an exchange of views and ideas and give practitioners a different perspective. This combining of information will allow a deeper insight to be gained of each child, which practitioners and parents can draw on to further enhance developmental opportunities (Forman and Fyfe, 1998).

In some early years environments, parent conferences take place on a more informal drop-in basis, though this may prove more difficult for establishing a two-directional communication that allows discussion of progress and plans for future direction. In most early years settings, parental conferences are already likely to take up a significant amount of time and there is likely to be a limit to allocating additional time. Many of these suggestions do not necessarily need to involve additional time. They are more about looking at what the current practice is and thinking about how this can be developed.

Learning portfolios

Hall *et al.* (2001) see documentation as an important vehicle in providing parents with access to a part of their child's life that is often not fully visible. As well as gaining an understanding of what their child has done, it can also be useful in helping parents to understand and see the purpose of maintaining records. One method of doing this is to construct a learning portfolio for children that is started on entry to the setting and moves with them. To increase partnership working, families should be encouraged to make contributions to the ongoing portfolio. Evidence can take a variety of forms, such as photographs, notes from observations, examples of the child's work or contributions from family members or practitioners about notable events. By encouraging the involvement of families in documentation they become an integral part of the process and can contribute to the discussion and debate about the development of their child, rather than documentation being used as a one-way communication method for informing or educating parents (Forman and Fyfe, 1998).

The foundation-stage profile was introduced in England in 2002–3 (QCA, 2002). Although this form of assessment is fully completed at the end of the reception year, a number of observations and range of evidence will be gathered throughout the foundation stage to assist practitioners with ensuring progression towards the Early Learning Goals (a set of statements in each of the six areas of learning that children work towards achieving at the end of the foundation stage)

(QCA/DfEE, 2000). This form of on-going assessment provides a number of opportunities to involve families in the process of gathering evidence and formulating plans for further learning (Ministry of Education, 1996; Forman and Fyfe, 1998; QCA/DfEE, 2000; Smidt, 2002).

Information sessions/workshops

A key element in the establishment of partnerships is the sharing of information. Planned sessions with families can be a useful forum to allow shared learning to take place. To ensure success careful thought needs to be given to the format of sessions to maximize parental participation. Edwards and Warin (1999) suggest that a reason for poor uptake at workshops is an over-emphasis on parents being told how to work in a teacher-directed style. So the challenge for practitioners is to create sessions that are based around equal participation and problem-solving with the aim of not doing more, but doing it better (Adams and Christenson, 2000). Workshops offer opportunities to provide information to parents about any aspect of learning or development. The choice of topic will depend on the needs and requests of parents. To meet these needs, and maximize attendance, consultation about the content is vital.

Parker (2002) describes an approach used to involve parents in their child's mark-making and promote a shared approach to learning. Initially, parents who had expressed an interest were approached individually (an approach that fathers often value) and from this a focus group of six to eight parents was formed. A series of sessions were offered, with the first used to introduce the project, the second and third to focus on each child's mark-making, two sessions that involved the children, and a final session to reflect on the workshops. In addition to useful discussions about mark-making and general issues, many parents were surprised by the capabilities of their child. Parents found this approach enabled them to interact, support and develop this area of learning further in the home environment (Tizard and Hughes, 2002). This form of workshop is useful for making parents aware that their support in early literacy development is important. Links can also be made to show parents how home-based resources and opportunities, such as access to varied print, reading with their child (simply by pointing at the words) or a family member reading and writing (acting as a role-model) are important prerequisites to the formal teaching of reading (Curtis, 1998).

In Chicago, increased parental involvement has been evident since 1988 in a variety of ways. One approach, The Parent Project, which is facilitated by a parent and teacher, involves a series of weekly two-hour workshops that begin by asking participants what their concerns are as parents. The topics generated are prioritized and produce the content for subsequent sessions. At each session the parents in the group explore an issue and generate a task around the content area to complete at home with their child, such as different art techniques to explore nature. The outcome of doing the task is discussed at the next session (Daniels, 1996). Alternatively, the focus can be on a specific topic, such as reading, personal, social and emotional education, or play-based learning. To ensure effectiveness it is important for practitioners to feel confident and have the necessary skills for this way of working. For less confident practitioners it may be more reassuring to work with a colleague as well as a parent in the initial sessions.

Daniels (1996) describes another approach, which begins with asking parents to think about their development as a reader and writer. Open questions are often given by the facilitator to support the process:

- What was your favourite book as a child?

- Can you remember a time when you really soared as a reader?

- What was the role of writing in your family?

- What was the best piece of writing you ever did?

After time for discussion, feedback from the group is invited about either positive or negative experiences. What usually comes out of this is that hurtful experiences often occurred in school and positive experiences occurred away from the educational setting. Giving parents copies of current approaches to teaching helps to develop links between their positive experiences and current research detailing good practice. Both of these approaches are useful in supporting parents in developing their knowledge of the curriculum and the types of approaches that can be beneficial in supporting their children, but in a way that is empowering, respectful of their role and values their experiences. When working in groups it is important not to assume that all parents will have the same level of literacy skills. To ensure each person is comfortable, choices about the role they take should be left to them, e.g. some people may prefer not to write, another may prefer to represent their ideas in pictures.

These approaches offer a framework that practitioners can draw on to develop information sessions and workshops in their setting. To support this further Dahlberg *et al.* (1999) offer guidance about what these sessions should and should not do:

- Sessions should be about families and practitioners working together in a reflective relationship.

- They should provide contextual information to parents that enables them to link effective support strategies to activities in the home environment, e.g. opportunities for communication during shopping trips.

- They should aim to recognize, promote and support the role of parents in the home environment.

Video-stimulated reflection

The use of video sequences offers opportunities for parents and practitioners to reflect on children's learning experiences. The Pen Green Centre for children and families in Northampton runs weekly drop-in groups where the child and parents come together. The practitioners (experienced in education, health and psychotherapy disciplines) who facilitate the group aim to encourage positive parent–child relationships. A method used to achieve this is videoing a child or child and parent interacting together and using this to produce a set of pictures. These can have language added to them to show the areas in which the child enjoys playing and the skills they use. The discussion around adding language supports parents and practitioners in careful thought and reflection about the activity that the child was engaged in and how it is promoting development; such as providing opportunities for increased levels of problem-solving or shared and sustained interaction to extend learning and support in the home learning environment (Moyles *et al.,* 2002; Sylva *et al.,* 2003). Occasionally a parent will be anxious about their child, perhaps because of a worry about their safety, happiness or well-being. A short video clip of the child engaged in activities and interacting with others can help to reassure parents that their child is well cared for and happy (Evans, 2002).

Hall *et al.* (2001) describe another approach using video clips to promote partnership with parents. To explore learning, they posed questions based on a video sequence of children engaged outdoors in growing and moving a large pumpkin. This was followed by a discussion to gain the perspective of parents and practitioners and to generate suggestions for extending learning further, which provided an excellent way of linking learning opportunities between home and the setting. Whalley (2001) suggests that using video clips that families have recorded in the home environment (and have agreed to show to other parents in the group) can be useful for showing the differences in learning between home and the setting. It can also provide an alternative discussion and reflection forum, but it is important to establish boundaries to ensure privacy and respect is maintained. Another benefit is that it can provide practitioners opportunities to see the child interacting with a parent who may not usually be able to attend the setting. In day-to-day interactions this can help to establish links that can be utilized to involve the child's parents in interactions in the setting, e.g. 'I saw you doing a jigsaw with your daddy, and it looked like good fun ...'.

Family events

Often family events are centred on fun days, concerts or other similar ideas. The principle can also be used to promote partnership with families in ways that support learning and development in a wider context. Rosenkoetter (2001), in response to a survey that found approximately a third of young children did not share reading or stories with their families, describes a community approach to address this – Bedtime Story Nights.

Once a month, parents and children gather for a 30-minute story or rhyme session. This is followed by a snack before going home to bed. Each month a different location (e.g. at the park, library or a nursing home), story reader (e.g. teacher, story teller, police officer) and theme (e.g. to link in a cultural event or fancy dress to match the story) can be used. Attempts can also be made to involve the community. As well as providing an event for families to attend together it gives opportunities for parents to observe useful techniques they can use at home. For example, letting the children lead, asking appropriate questions about the story, using props to engage interest and animating the story telling. As the event takes place in the evening it may allow involvement of parents who cannot attend daytime events because of their work commitments.

Newsletters

Regular newsletters can be a useful way of maintaining contact with families and the community about current issues, events and achievements. To ensure a representative approach in newsletters, contributions should be included from the setting, families and the community, and distributed to the same wide body of people. It is very easy for newsletters to become a vehicle for transmitting day-to-day issues, dates, holiday information and similar points. This is a valid and important use for them, but in addition there is potential for them to be used in a far more integrated and inclusive way. This can include contributions from family members, a review of a recent information session, details of a recent family event, coverage of cultural festivals and information about new services, written by the person or group who experienced the event. If necessary, some simple guidance points can be given by the editing group to support contributors. To help collate information and spread the workload, as well as promoting partnership, it can be useful to have a small editorial group of perhaps two to four people formed from a variety of sources, such as family members, practitioners and administration staff. If necessary, this group can also provide simple guidance to support contributors.

To maintain contact with family members, practitioners can explore the benefits of information and communication technology. E-mail can be a useful method of communicating with families, especially extended family or a non-resident parent. By using group facilities on e-mail accounts it is relatively straightforward to send a message to all families. Other potential uses of information and communication technology are constructing websites for your setting or running an online discussion board. Practitioners may have reservations about the use of information and communication technology because of access or privacy issues. These are valid concerns, and need addressing, but as further advances are made it is likely that the use of communication technology will become even more common and access issues will reduce.

Setting information sheets

For parents, many aspects of the organization may be confusing. For example, the different arrangement of rooms in the early years environment, especially if there are reasons why their child may not have moved to a particular room by what is deemed as the *starting age*. To support parents, short handouts that detail the organization and routine of the room, and explain stages of development and link it to the practice of the room, can be useful and reassuring (Evans, 2002). This will also provide parents with ideas and suggestions that they may find useful to support interactions and play with their child at home.

Home learning

Children learn a great deal from home, particularly from birth to the age of three. This is primarily achieved because of family support and needs to be acknowledged. When children move into an educational setting the importance of input from home remains. Practitioners and parents need to work together to help children develop the skills necessary to benefit from the different experiences available to them, to help them explore and express their feelings, and learn about their place in the group. An effective partnership with the family is vital in allowing practitioners access to the unseen pictures that make up the child's life (Roberts, 2002).

A frequent comment heard from parents is that they want to support their child at home but do not always feel confident in doing this and feel additional guidance is needed (Epstein and Saunders, 2002). To offer more support to parents, practitioners can provide resources focused on the requirements of parents. As well as supporting parents it can improve home–school communication, which has also been identified as a way of improving trust (Adams and Christenson 2000). Organizations that support parents produce a range of literature that can provide concise and relevant guidance. Parentline Plus, a United Kingdom registered charity, produce a variety of accessible and informative information sheets to support parents, as shown in Figures 7 and 8.

Storysacks (which consist of a large cloth bag, a picture book to stimulate language, soft toys to represent some of the characters, and props linked to the story) have become a popular resource for settings to make available to families to borrow. The aim of the sacks is to provide opportunities for families to engage in discussion around a story and to stimulate use of a wide range of vocabulary (Basic Skills Agency, 2003). Although this has the basis for supporting home learning, a repeated comment from parents is that they are told of the need to read to their children but not why it is important or the types of strategies that they can use. Again, settings can respond to this by producing information guides that can justify to parents the reasons behind this request, as shown in Figure 8. To add a more personal touch to information sheets it can help to have two versions: one using female pronouns and the other male. There is sometimes a tendency to avoid the use of technical words in information for parents (e.g. phoneme), but as long as these are explained clearly it can help to involve families in the actual language processes used around learning and be a more empowering experience (Jordan *et al.*, 1998).

Learning comes naturally to babies and young children. Day by day they are growing physically, emotionally, socially and mentally, developing their intelligence and understanding about the world around them. Parents, and other family members, play a vital role in helping young children learn: they are a child's first teachers.

How to support young children's learning and development

Talk and sing to children from day one. It will help them develop their memory of sounds and later of words.

Be guided by the child: observe what she or he is able to do, and encourage her or him gradually to build on what they are able to do.

Accept that each child grows and develops at his or her own pace. Avoid comparisons with other children, and try not to put a child under pressure to do anything she or he is not ready to do. This applies equally to walking, to potty training and to reading.

Encourage reading. Talk about the pictures in baby books and read to your child from an early age. Encourage them by having books, magazines and newspapers in the home. Let them see you and other family members reading them. Pointing to and saying words as you travel together, at parks, in shops, also helps.

Feed children's natural curiosity. Give toddlers and young children a variety of safe and interesting objects to explore.

Play with your children sometimes. It's an opportunity to show your interest and delight in their discoveries and achievements.

Try to give toddlers and young children space to enjoy physical movement and games – running, skipping, climbing, playing ball games. Parks and playgrounds are ideal.

Consider joining a parent and toddlers club, a playgroup, toy library or nursery. These, too, are good places to meet other parents, and help a child develop social skills in readiness for school.

Enjoy everyday activities together. These are opportunities to talk about things, name them and identify words.

Figure 7: Parentline Plus

Parent Partnership in the Early Years

<u>Reading Aloud</u>

Reading aloud to your child will help to...
- Allow him to begin to understand the reading process
- Provide knowledge and experience of different areas
- Build his vocabulary and knowledge of language
- Show that reading is pleasurable and fun

(Hall and Moats 2000)

Some ideas on making reading aloud enjoyable

One to two years...
Provide a range of books for him to choose from in different parts of the house, such as the play box, plastic coated for the bathroom and bedroom. Try to respond to his request to be read to, especially if he brings a book to you.

Try to make reading times fun, perhaps saying repeat words together or introducing a song. Young children will often end reading prematurely; it can be better to accept it. He may also try to turn the pages too quickly; a way around this is to make up a story to match the picture. This time talking will be really valuable.

Two years and above...
Having a routine, perhaps at a story at bedtime, is good and can also help in getting ready to go to sleep. You may find he has a favourite reading spot, perhaps lying on his bed or sat in a special chair. It can be enjoyable to have time for reading with children together, if you have more than one child, or one adult reads to a child one night and swaps the next.

Using props or puppets can be fun and provide opportunities to think about naming people and objects and opportunities to show and respond to feelings, which can also generate some talk between you both about the story. Modelling different language patterns is both fun and educational, e.g. different voices for animals.

To support the development of children's language and reading it is helpful for them to see adults modelling the reading process and see words in a variety of situations (e.g. books, signs and labels in shops). Skills that are associated with successful reading during school years are having an understanding of the rime in words (e.g. beak and weak), finding the initial phoneme (the smallest unit of sound, e.g. <u>t</u>o, sh<u>oe</u>) of words and segmenting words into syllables. As well as providing a good foundation for the development of these skills reading aloud also presents opportunities for one-to-one interaction, which has emotional and social benefits as well as educational. Reading aloud with him will make a difference.

(Harris and Butterworth 2002)

Figure 8: Reading aloud information guide

Book and toy libraries provide another useful resource to involve parents, share resources and work in partnership. As discussed, the amount of time available for practitioners to be involved in all initiatives is limited. A group of parents will often happily take responsibility for collecting resources, and organizing and administering the lending of toys and books. Parents may also decide that additional resources would be beneficial and take on the role of fund-raising to achieve this.

Involving the family and community in the learning environment

For families to feel part of the educational setting there needs to be recognition of them in the learning environment. Including pictures of the family in the setting can achieve this and show children that their family are valued. A book, with each family asked to fill a page, can be constructed and displayed in the setting for children, practitioners and other families to look at (Hilliard *et al.,* 2001). As well as helping the community to get to know each other this can also provide a valuable learning resource for the setting. Displays showing family and community members can be used in entrance areas to form part of a welcoming display, perhaps integrated with an information board for families. To ensure children are involved, some thought about the positioning of information is important to ensure accessibility for all (Gandini, 1998).

To bridge the gap between the setting and home,

children can be encouraged to share their work with parents in an informal way (Hilliard *et al.,* 2001). As well as sending work home, opportunities to invite family members into settings are helpful in sharing learning. Again, this can be informal, or at a pre-planned open session where family members are encouraged to call in and observe the routine, interact with children and engage with practitioners. Educational visits can be useful for involving parents, particularly fathers, and often rely on their help to enable them to take place. To assist families, early notice should be given, if possible, to allow alterations to work or other commitments to be made. Educational visits can also provide invaluable opportunities to talk and interact with parents who attend the setting less frequently.

Additional opportunities for involvement in the learning environment include family members assisting with an activity or session, reading with children, taking on a role as a governor, fund-raising or helping to run a service, e.g. toy library (Curtis, 1998; Daper and Duffy, 2001). At the start of a term, settings can make requests to families about the help they need through the newsletter and by displaying requests on a family information board. As well as providing advance notice to families to allow them to plan their time, it can also give settings access to skills within families to support and extend the variety of learning opportunities offered to children. Examples of skills that family members have shared include brick laying, building bird boxes, making pots, erecting tents and growing vegetables, many of which are often not possible without this additional support.

Informal opportunities for interaction

It is easy to overlook informal opportunities for communicating with families, but they can be immensely useful in developing effective partnerships, particularly with fathers. Hilliard *et al.* (2001) discuss how actually asking parents what you can do for them can lead to a more open relationship and provide vital information to practitioners about responding to actual rather than perceived needs. Small issues, such as making a greeting personal, taking the time to follow-up on an earlier conversation, or asking for an opinion about something, are important. This communicates to parents that how they are feeling matters, their input is valued and they are respected. Informal exchanges are also valuable in building a rapport and can offer opportunities to learn about family culture, composition and interests (Jordan *et al.,* 1998), which is important in developing respect, providing a supportive environment and working in partnership. Eldridge (2001) suggests that another method of utilizing less formal communication is to send a short note home to parents to identify a couple of ways to support their child with a skill they are acquiring, such as counting, learning a rhyme or playing a new cooperative game. This is useful as it involves each parent in their child's learning (as it is addressed to the adults who parent the child) and avoids any feelings that they have done something wrong.

Key worker system

A key worker system is useful in supporting a child's adjustment to the setting. Additionally, parents can find having a consistent practitioner to chat issues over with useful and supportive. With the expansion of early years provision, the skills of practitioners are often varied and comprehensive (Rolfe *et al.*, 2003). Therefore, the operation of a key worker system can offer benefits to parents and children and utilize and develop the skills practitioners have. With appropriate support and training key workers can facilitate support and exchange of information through regular informal group meetings with their link families. Throughout the time a child attends the setting they become the key point of contact and support.

Transition into school

Moving into school is a major transition for a child and their family. For families, important issues are the management of change and ensuring that their child is secure. For practitioners, it is to recognize and respond to the needs of each child and support their transition. For children, the importance of developing friendships in the setting is a central need (Perry and Dockett, 2003). When children are moving to a new setting, encouragement and support from practitioners is important for providing and maintaining continuity. The transition from an early years setting to school is an important time for parents. To aid this process, regular contact with transition partners and opportunities for all the family to be involved will allow them to be confident that their child will manage the transition (Griebel and Niesel, 2002).

A key approach to preventing misunderstandings is to share information and maintain two-way communication (Neuman, 2002). It is also important for children as it helps them to adjust, leads to less problems and makes families feel welcome to the new environment (Epstein and Saunders, 2002). Effective strategies to facilitate a smooth transition include:

- communicating to parents that their child is ready for school by stressing the competencies they have;

- organizing information sessions for families that are attended by practitioners from the current and new settings;

- inviting teachers from the school into the early years setting to participate in play and social activities;

- organizing transition sessions where parents and children can visit the school environment to gain familiarity;

- communicating information to the school to ensure that the grouping of children in the new setting helps the maintenance of friendships;

- having effective communication systems for the transfer of key information to the school, e.g. child likes and dislikes, any concerns in relation to development, and family information that parents want to be passed on.

4

Working with Fathers

The role of fathers in families

Traditionally the majority of childcare within families was usually undertaken by women, but since the 1980s there has been a shift in both societal expectations and the policy agenda to encourage increased participation of fathers in parenting and educational settings, especially for young children (McBride *et al.*, 2001). Prior to this much of the debate was centred on how fathers could provide financially for the family and act as good role models for their children. Little attention was given to the caring role of fathers within families (Lewis, 2002). Although changes in working patterns and family responsibility have altered, the Equal Opportunities Commission (2003) found that the idea of the 'breadwinning role' for many fathers remains crucial, with 86 per cent of fathers working full-time (compared to 31 per cent of mothers). Hidden in these statistics, however, is a great level of variety, which emphasizes the importance of seeing fathers as a diverse group.

Fathers are increasingly moving towards greater involvement in the social role of fathering. This includes participating in varied activities, including attending antenatal classes and childbirth, and increased involvement with their child's education. In response to this there has been an increase in the range and number of classes devoted to exploring fathering, but this has also had the affect of adding to the complexity of the role of fathers (Hearn, 2002). Although these challenges are likely to provide more opportunities for father involvement, they also highlight difficulties for men. Hearn (2002) highlights that this new role, often referred to as *new man*, has limited role models for men to learn from and follow. This makes it likely that fathers will need to map out this new territory independently or perhaps with others in a similar position, a view supported by Macleod (2000). Even without such changes, some fathers (and mothers) may not have had good role models from their own fathers (Frieman and Berkeley, 2002).

At a general level this has led to a perceived view of greater father involvement. Even though the amount of time fathers are spending with children has risen, the increase has only been gradual (Pleck, 1997; McBride *et al.*, 2001) and can often be linked to specific tasks, such as shopping, putting children to bed or an increased role at weekends, but this may be linked to employment issues (Hearn, 2002). It is suggested that fathers fall into one of four groups, with most fathers falling into the two middle groups (Equal Opportunities Commission, 2002):

- enforcer – involved in day-to-day care and act as a role model for setting clear rules;

- entertainer – often entertaining while partner carries out household roles;

- useful – entertains but also takes a share in household tasks and childcare;

- fully-involved – parental roles virtually interchangeable.

There is also a clear correlation between work and involvement among fathers, with a reduction in contact with children as working hours increase (Flouri and Buchanan, 2003). However, the quality of the contact is as important, if not more so, than the quantity (Levine 1993; Jaffee *et al.*, 2003). Younger men in particular are expressing a preference to participate more fully in family life (Equal Opportunities Commission, 2003), which reinforces the importance of establishing effective and supportive partnerships in educare settings.

For children, there can be significant benefits to father involvement, including greater levels of well-being, empathy and an internal locus of control (taking responsibility for own actions and able to control own behaviour) (Levine, 1993; Jaffee *et al.*, 2003). These factors are associated with emotional development (Smith *et al.*, 2003) and establishing and maintaining friendships, which is associated with a better attitude towards school and increased attainment in later years (Hartup, 1998). For some children this may not be the case. Jaffee *et al.* (2003) highlight that for fathers who engage in high levels of antisocial behaviour, the more time they spend with their children the greater the likelihood of the child having behaviour problems. Although father presence can be hard to quantify, this again highlights the complex interplay of factors in families that impact on child development.

Although it is not possible for practitioners to influence all aspects of father and child interaction it does show how their role in promoting and support-ing fathers as parents is both necessary and important. It can also be argued that this is particularly important in early years, as fathers are more likely to be involved in parenting younger children and the earlier that involvement is estab-lished the more likely it is to continue throughout the childhood years (Pryor and Rodgers, 2001; Knijn and Selten, 2002; Flouri and Buchanan, 2003).

Barriers to father involvement

Although there have been examples of successful programmes to promote the involvement of fathers, many practitioners have found that, even after sustained effort, numbers have remained low. A number of barriers have been identified that can either prevent or hinder father involvement. Turbiville *et al.* (2000) found that discussion of parental involvement was often gender neutral but this was still often perceived as meaning mother, which can leave the father feeling rebuffed. An example of a simple action is when a child is ill; the first person contacted is usually the mother (Equal Opportunities Commission 2003). Another example of a patron-izing interaction is a father being asked to take messages to their child's mother or mothers asked to confirm information previously given by the father.

This is likely to have a devaluing effect, as mothers will usually share this with fathers afterwards. Although this may be the preference of the family, this should not be assumed before asking.

Other barriers to involvement include longer working hours, inflexible work patterns, job insecurity, low income and social exclusion, all of which can contribute to fathers feeling a sense of failure (Equal Opportunities Commission, 2002). Historically there has been a focus on the role of the mother in child development theories (e.g. Freud's interactional theory and Bowlby's attachment theory, which identified the significance of the mother's role in attachment). Even though revisions have been made to many of the early findings, the overriding maternal focus on interactions with practitioners may still impact to some degree (Schaffer, 1998). Nurturing and teaching, which are significant parts of the routine and roles in early years settings, have traditionally been seen as women's work (Macleod, 2000). This can be as damaging for women as it can be for men, in terms of status, opportunities and income, and needs to be tackled (Mayo, 1998; Equal Opportunities Commission, 2002).

From the evidence, one of the challenges facing fathers is the need to balance economic and other commitments with their parenting role. Recent changes to paternity leave entitlement in the United Kingdom have provided fathers with two weeks paid maternity leave. Although an improvement, in comparison to other countries this is relatively poor. In the 1980s and 1990s, central government's policy on fathers focused on financial support, which although important should be seen alongside social support as well (Lewis, 2002). In contrast, Sweden have a whole range of polices to both support and promote the role of fathers. These include 'daddy month' (part of the paternity leave package), the formation of government working groups to promote and support father involvement, and increased automatic levels of custody rights from birth. These have the aim of supporting and nurturing the role of fathers (Bergman and Hobson, 2002). The lack of emphasis in the UK on promoting the positive roles of fathers in families has potentially negative consequences for fathers, their partners and children (Knijn and Selten, 2002). Early years practitioners can help address this by working in partnership with fathers.

Levine (1993) has identified a number of factors that fathers feel may limit involvement. These include fear of exposing inadequacy; ambivalence of setting staff members towards fathers; mothers being the main communicator/decision-maker about educare services; and inappropriate programme design and delivery. Consequently, these factors may limit the level of involvement, even though fathers may want to participate. Practitioners can also have doubts about parental involvement (from both fathers and mothers). This can be related to the potential for negative interactions between them and parents, perceived lack of parental skills or the fear of parents having unhelpful views or opinions towards early years settings. Ambivalence from the mother's viewpoint towards father involvement has also been identified as impacting negatively on father involvement (Levine, 1993).

Many of the principles that work for promoting the involvement of mothers can be applied to fathers but may need to be focused in a different manner. This is reinforced by the experiences of many settings who have found take-up and participation in events to be extremely low among fathers. Macleod (2000) reports on a series of workshops focusing on working with parents to help them improve their skills and support children. Out of 169 participants, only six were men, five of whom dropped out. One of the reasons cited for deterring fathers' involvement is the implicit culture surrounding early years settings that it is mothers who support the educational setting. Frieman and Berkeley (2002) suggest that practitioners, who are often predominantly female, may find it harder to relate to fathers, although fathers did not see other men on the staff as making it easier to participate (Turbiville *et al.*, 2000). Positively, this suggests that barriers are not necessarily constructed by the gender of practitioners. Sumsion (2000) argues that all practitioners, regardless of gender, need to negotiate their role with children, parents and colleagues. So potentially the idea that having more male practitioners is necessary to increase father involvement could be too simplistic. More positively, an increased level of father involvement is potentially a goal attainable by all early years settings.

Promoting the involvement of fathers

Informal involvement of fathers can present significant opportunities to develop partnership working.

Parent Partnership in the Early Years

Fathers often take on the role of bringing and collecting children from the early years setting, which can provide perfect opportunities for including fathers in decision-making processes and be the basis of *hooking* fathers into activities (Levine, 1993). To maximize these informal opportunities, practitioners need to develop confidence in approaching fathers, commenting on what their child has been involved in and laying the basis for the father to offer feedback. Additionally, this can be useful in laying the basis for a trusting relationship. Fathers appreciate being personally asked to participate and feeling as though their effort is appreciated (Turbiville *et al.*, 2000).

The timing of events or workshops is significant as it can interfere with work and family schedules that fathers may not be able to alter (Turbiville *et al.*, 2000; Frieman and Berkeley, 2002). If a specific event is being organized it is likely to attract more fathers if it is scheduled for the evening or at the weekend (Equal Opportunities Commission, 2003). For practitioners, this can place additional demands on their time, but if the event is to succeed working practices need to be flexible, especially as such events are likely to occur fairly infrequently. This flexibility in recognizing the other demands on fathers is another method of showing that the setting is responding to the needs of parents and will help to contribute to developing successful partnerships (Frieman and Berkeley, 2002). Informal contact with fathers, as discussed earlier, can provide a useful opportunity for asking fathers when the most suitable time would be for activities to be scheduled to allow greater levels of participation.

Groups or workshops for fathers can be a useful vehicle for supporting them in their role as parents, especially for first-time fathers who may feel they lack experience. In practice, many practitioners may have found attendance by fathers to be low, which raises questions about the approach used. Groups aimed at fathers are more likely to be successful if they are given an educational, rather than a feeling, aim (Frieman and Berkeley, 2002). For example, sessions aimed at developing play skills or helping children to gain an understanding of the world rather than helping children develop friendships are better attended. In many respects, this represents a move away from the 'caring and sharing' approach to an educational focus (Macleod, 2000).

The initial hurdle to overcome is to encourage fathers to attend the first session, especially as many fathers may have anxieties about exposing any inadequacy they find in their parenting role. An important part of parenting though is learning, and often the most successful learning comes from making mistakes. Practitioners need to capture the ethos of this in their communication with fathers by stressing the collaborative and supportive nature of groups and the opportunities to learn together. It should be stressed to fathers, perhaps through informal conversations, that children learn to respect a father who makes mistakes and corrects them and this is likely to be a valuable source of modelling for the child to learn from (Frieman and Berkeley, 2002). Levine (1993) suggests that reaching fathers first as men, by encouraging involvement in an activity they feel confident with, and then building on this, may be useful. Allowing fathers to choose how they become involved in ways that allow them to respond in a way that is not threatening to their own gender role is likely to be more successful (Coates, 2003). This could involve asking fathers to participate in the setting with an activity they feel comfortable with, such as:

- reading to one or two children;

- coming on a trip or visit;

- working with a small group of children in the garden;

- supporting children with use of audio, video or computer equipment;

- organizing a sport game (for children or other fathers);

- drawing on a particular skill or hobby they have.

When asked, fathers identified their five preferred types of participation as family activities, 'daddy and me' programmes (children and fathers doing things together), activities involving both parents learning about future issues, child development sessions involving both parents, and sporting events (Turbiville et al., 2000). Highest levels of father participation have been seen in events that involve family participation. This suggests that sole sessions for fathers may not be appropriate, especially in the early stages of developing partnerships. This could be related to working fathers not wanting to divert the time they have away from their family and any fear they may have in exposing perceived inadequacies in their parenting role. If the decision is made to organize a group for fathers, consideration of the venue is important. Traditional venues, such as the educational setting, can be seen as places where nurturing and chat takes place and may not be an ideal setting to make fathers feel at ease. To overcome this it may be decided that an alternative setting, which is suitable for both fathers and practitioners, is needed to chat about issues related to fathering and developing positive relationships with their children (Macleod, 2000).

In communication with parents, Frieman and Berkeley (2002) state the importance of having fathers' views (as well as mothers') in newsletters and correspondence with the child's home. An approach to this is to include a column written by a male (if in post) and female member of the setting. Alternatively, contributions could be requested from parents in the setting, about issues in general, child development or any other relevant topics. Making efforts to ensure that contributions are balanced in terms of mother and father input will also communicate the message that fathers' views are important and valued. Other useful information to include in newsletters to promote father involvement can be details about affordable education visits or suitable toys for children at different ages, as fathers have identified these as preferred options for increased involvement. For settings, the benefits of promoting this type of involvement may not be immediately evident as they are carried out away from the educational setting. For children, though, the benefits could be long-lasting.

Efforts also need to be made to ensure that written communication reaches all parents, which includes non-resident fathers who still maintain parental responsibility (clarification should be sought in individual cases). This is particularly important for families who have recently separated, as this can involve parents adapting to changes in their parenting role. In addition, children generally continue to see the non-resident parent as part of the family group: a situation the educational setting needs to support. In these circumstances, electronic forms of communication could provide a suitable means of exchanging information, particularly to support the parent in the early stages of the transition and help fathers maintain a sense of involvement in their child's education and care (Chaboudy et al., 2001).

As discussed, evidence shows that for the vast majority of children involvement from their father has a beneficial impact and is important (Featherstone, 2003). Many factors impact on father involvement, including their level of education, employment status, the number of children in the family and relationship with their partner (Flouri and Buchanan, 2003). Although these are mainly outside the control of the early years setting, there are many areas where practitioners can have a significant and positive impact. Practitioners can offer support to fathers in developing a range of skills to support and interact effectively with their children, and the earlier that this involvement begins the more beneficial it is likely to be.

It is also important to remember that the quality of involvement is the key, not the quantity. Much of the benefit that practitioners can bring about may not be visible because it is carried out away from the setting. This is particularly relevant with fathers, as the level of interaction they have with their child may be much greater than their involvement in the setting would suggest. The most effective support for fathers is likely to come from a mutual partnership between the father and practitioner, where each has empathy and understanding towards the other and responds supportively. A challenge for practitioners is to ensure that each father views themselves as an involved carer rather than a failed provider (Equal Opportunities Commission, 2003).

It is important to see each father individually, recognize the different issues he has and aim to respond to these in an appropriate and effective manner (Trowell, 2002). The life experiences of each child will vary. Children may have a father who may be the sole carer, a member of another ethnic group, a gay parent or absent from the home. In the same way that it is vital to respect and value each child it is necessary to apply this to each parent, which is a central challenge in maintaining an effective partnership with each parent.

5

Creating Partnerships: Overcoming Barriers

Although practitioners can take many steps to maintain effective partnerships, it is likely that there will be occasions when barriers either exist or develop. An awareness of the type of issues that can lead to actual or perceived barriers between practitioners and families can help to either avoid or overcome problems. Neuman (2002) suggests that common barriers can occur for cultural, attitudinal, language and logistical reasons. As well as fathers, groups that can feel excluded include families from ethnic minorities, refugee families, families headed by gay parents, and families where children have disabilities (Braun, 2001). It is not possible or realistic to suggest that every potential barrier can be covered in this section, but the aim is to provide an overview for practitioners to gain an understanding of common issues that can lead to difficulties, and from this gain a greater awareness of how to respond to ensure they are overcome.

Valuing diversity: creating an inclusive setting

Staff in some early years settings reflect the diversity

of their communities, while staff from other settings may represent one or two cultures but operate in diverse and wider communities. When people hear the term ethnicity it is often assumed that it relates to skin colour and the place a person was born. Ethnicity encompasses characteristics, including family origin, appearance, language, family structure, religion, food, music, literature and gender roles (Storkey, 1991). Within this range of characteristics it is likely that there will be similarities among people from the same ethnic group but there will also be many differences. This reminds us of the need to recognize difference and not treat all families with the same ethnicity as a homogenous group (Jordan *et al.*, 1998; Thompson, 2001). It is also important to remember that each of us belongs to an ethnic group, although there are significant differences in the size of each group. The need to value ethnicity and see the benefits of diversity is vital, as Thompson (2001) describes the long-lasting effects that racism can have on families:

Racism is a powerful force in society. It subjects one portion of society – black and ethnic minority groups – to oppression, degradation and discrimination on the grounds that they are deemed to be inferior, by virtue of biology and/or culture … (p. 76)

To promote involvement of all parents, the organization and curriculum of the setting need to send a strong message. The Curriculum Guidance for England states the importance of reflecting the children's homes and community (QCA/DfEE, 2000). In New Zealand, the Te Whariki Curriculum is built on four broad principles, one of which is the family and community and the integrated part they play with the setting (Ministry of Education, 1996). Jordan *et al.* (1998) state the importance of building trust with parents of all cultures and the need for practitioners to learn about customs and traditions. One way for practitioners to do this is to attend cultural awareness events that are organized by different ethnic or religious communities. For example, in Sheffield the Muslim community run an event that practitioners can attend to increase their awareness and understanding of the faith. Events such as this can provide an insight into how cultural and race can impact on bringing up children in society (Hirst and Joseph, 1998).

Practitioners need to be aware of their personal beliefs and practices to help avoid actions that could lead to unintentional racism. Managers of early education and care settings need to take a role in this by ensuring that polices and practices acknowledge, value and celebrate difference. Practitioners need access to appropriate support, information and training to ensure practice is anti-discriminatory. Greenman (2001) summarizes this well by recognizing the demands this places on practitioners but also the benefits of empowering all parents:

Full parent partnerships that recognize and respect the common bonds and the ways that families and children are different build a community of caring and learning (p. 59)

It is important for practitioners to take time to build a trusting relationship with all parents and recognize their role within the partnership. Caplan *et al.* (1997)

support this by stating that polices and strategies need to develop attitudes that reflect the diversity of the community and stress the importance of developing awareness to help each partner to understand the different perspectives and dispositions of those in the relationship. To set this in context, a setting may approach a parent who they do not know well and ask if they would come and talk to the children about an aspect of their culture. Although well-meaning, this attaches a particular identity to the parent and assumes that they are familiar with the particular cultural practice. It can also suggest that coverage of ethnic and cultural issues takes place at specific times only and are not threaded though the curriculum. This type of interaction runs the risk of reinforcing the idea of ethnicity almost as something that is detached and different to the heritage of the local community rather than part of it.

Gay- and lesbian-headed families

Parents usually feel anxious when their child first starts to attend an early years setting but, after talking with practitioners and seeing their child settle, this usually begins to recede quickly. For gay and lesbian parents, anxiety and stress may continue because of concerns over disclosing their sexuality to the setting and the impact that this may have on the child (Casper and Schultz, 1999). Although it is unlikely that any practitioner will treat a child less favourably because of their family environment, many gay and lesbian parents are likely to have experienced some form of prejudice because of their sexual orientation. So, understandably, they are likely to be anxious in new situations. Practitioners may express implicit or explicit concerns about the impact on children of living with gay or lesbian parents. Concern may relate to children's gender formation, sense of identity or later sexual orientation. Research evidence has explored each of these areas and has consistently found such concern to be unfounded. The important factors in determining outcomes for children are based on the ability of parents to offer a loving, supportive and stimulating home environment, not the sexual orientation of parents (Patterson and Redding, 1996; Roberts, 2001). Casper and Schultz (1999) identify a number of steps that practitioners can take to form effective partnerships with gay and lesbian parents:

- Be aware of the kinds of language used in the setting. Try to use terms that are inclusive when communicating with large groups of children, such as parent or parents rather than mummy and daddy.

- Consider what procedures and support can be offered to parents new to the setting to help them feel comfortable in disclosing their sexuality.

- Review documentation completed by parents. Do forms include terms that are specific to hetero-sexual parents (e.g. mother and father)? Consider using more inclusive terms, such as parent or guardian. Repeat these terms to gain details of a second parent if present.

- Are the experiences of all families reflected in the setting? For example, do all photographs show a mother and father? If so how can changes be made to reflect and celebrate the diversity of all families in the community?

- Are steps taken to encourage all parents to become involved?

- Does informal communication make assumptions? For example, referring to one parent as father and using a different term for the other.

- Have the team considered how questions that could arise from children will be dealt with? Will they take account of the levels of understanding of the children? Will they provide an affirming and supportive response?

- Are there opportunities for the team to discuss their feelings about children being raised by gay or lesbian parents? This is important as it will impact on individual practice and interactions with families.

Creating positive attitudes

For many parents, early years practitioners may be the first group of people associated with education that they have contact with. It is likely that some children may take longer to integrate into the setting, engage actively in the opportunities available and interact with the other children and adults. This can present challenges for parents, as they may blame themselves for any difficulties, begin to question whether their child has a special need or feel apprehensive about discussing this with practitioners. The longer the difficulty persists the more anxious the family is likely to become. Todd and Higgins (1998) describe a scenario where a difference of opinion occurred over a child: the setting seeing the issue as a behaviour problem; the parent as a learning difficulty. Figure 9, written by a parent, clearly shows how an inappropriate approach in making parents aware of difficulties can have a destructive impact on the development of an effective partnership.

Greenman (2001) acknowledges that individual differences will occur, but it is vital for parents to feel they have power in the situation. If parents feel empowered this is likely to lead to quality care, gain support from parents in responding to the situation, and result in better outcomes for each child. This can be particularly important if parents are asked for permission to seek the advice of outside support agencies. It is also important to consider the educational experiences that parents may have had as children. If these were difficult it is not likely that they will immediately have trust in education and care settings. As discussed earlier, attributes that can have positive influences on practitioner–parent relationships include warmth, openness, sensitivity, flexibility, reliability and accessibility (Keyes, 2002). Practitioners can draw on these skills to guide their communication with parents, particularly in early contact, as this is a significant period in setting the foundations for working in partnership.

An overriding need with every family is for them to

I took my child to nursery every day, feeling it was important for him to learn some social skills before school. I got a place at our local nursery and was very excited about him starting. At first everything seemed ok, but after a while Lewis was not enjoying his daily sessions as much. Then after one session the teacher said she would like a word so I stayed behind. She told me Lewis had been very disruptive, had been shouting and been a general nuisance. I told her I would speak to Lewis and left feeling very surprised. After speaking to Lewis I felt sure it would not happen again, but things seemed to get worse and worse. On a daily basis when she saw me standing in the line, in front of all the other parents she would say 'I need a word, mum; he's been very disruptive again' in a loud voice, which was very embarrassing. One day his teacher spoke to me and told me that she had been a pre-school teacher for thirteen years, and had never come across a child as disruptive and badly behaved as Lewis. I was very upset and concerned about my child and began to think about what he would be like at school. From these daily conversations I do not remember even one positive comment. In the end I felt that was causing a triangle of stress for myself, the teacher and Lewis, so I stopped sending him. The teacher offered me no advice on what I could do and I felt very let down. Later that year Lewis was offered a place at another nursery. I felt very reluctant to send him but after a meeting with the new teachers I felt that it was important. I decided to tell the new setting what had happened previously, but they were not concerned, assured me they worked 100 per cent on praise and encouragement and said to wait and see. By the end of the first session I was feeling very nervous expecting to be called in but this was not the case. After him being there for a few weeks I nervously approached the teachers. They told me they had only had to speak to Lewis on a few occasions for very minor reasons since being there and that they had not needed to tell me as it had been dealt with. At first I felt very confused after the last teacher had experienced so many problems, but as the good reports increased I started to feel angry and let down by the previous nursery. I still feel upset that his first experience of nursery was so judgemental and unsupportive. This nursery was the first place Lewis was out of my care and I felt it let him down badly.

Figure 9: A parent's perspective on negative communication

be seen (and for them to feel that they are seen) as competent and legitimate, i.e. that they are capable of providing an environment that is conducive to promoting the development of their child (Bailey, 2001). Although practitioners may disagree with the actions or choices a family make, interactions need to remain positive and respectful. Other factors that impact on partnership between practitioners and parents are the degree of match between the values and culture of parents, the education setting and the locality. For example, levels of poverty and employment affect how each partner sees their role. From one perspective, practitioners may see significant differences as impacting negatively on the formation of effective partnerships, but the greater the effort made to bridge the divide the more likely it is that children, families and the setting will benefit (Keyes, 2002). Bailey (2001) develops this further by suggesting self-reflection questions that can contribute to developing positive attitudes and support strategies for all families:

- Did practitioners engage in helpful practice, such as active listening to clarify concerns?

- Was the family supported to be a central agent of intervention and change to help develop their child's level of competence?

- Was the family supported in being an advocate for their situation?

- Was the family supported in maintaining responsibility for the situation and taking a central role in guiding the action to resolve it?

Resolving conflict

Inevitably, conflicts will occur in any early years setting. This could be because a parent is concerned about a routine, an aspect of practice, or the way a situation has been brought to their attention or dealt with. From the practitioner's perspective they may be concerned about an issue concerning the child or family. Realistically, it is unlikely that conflict can be avoided totally and may in fact present opportunities for practitioners and families to work together to explore ways the situation can be avoided in the future and lead to improvements in practice. Keyser (2001) outlines a set of principles that practitioners can draw on to make this more likely:

- **Think about the choice of words**. If a child has been behaving aggressively or being disruptive this needs to be raised with the parent, but avoiding blame is important. For example, a practitioner says, 'Joe has had some disagreements today with his friends and hit out a couple of times'. Parents will realize from this statement that there is a problem without being told that their child has upset other children.

- **Listen attentively to show respect for the parent's point of view**. Even though a situation may have occurred in the setting, parents can often provide an insight that may help to explain certain behaviour. For example, if a child has been hitting out at other children it may be that they are having difficulties with friendships or have been having difficulties with behaviour at home.

Practitioners need to resolve situations in collaboration with the family, as they are likely to have information that will help.

- **Show understanding for the parent's perspective and aim to find common ground**. Parents will almost always be supportive and assist in trying to resolve a situation. It is important though to work in partnership with them. For example, if a child has been unkind to other children they may have told their parent that they have been called names or excluded by other children. The common ground is resolving the situation, but it would also be an opportunity to work on resolving hurtful behaviour that is occurring among some groups of children. By working closely with parents, not only will the individual situation be resolved, but there will also be opportunities to work on developing social relationships for all children.

- **State your ideas, opinion and experience**. It is completely acceptable and likely to be reassuring to parents to give your input on resolving the situation. When doing this, practitioners need to take ownership of the idea, e.g. 'In my experience ...', or 'I believe ...', or 'In our setting ...'. The important issue though is to maintain two-way communication and not to dominate the discussion.

- **Clarify the problem and invite solutions**. Once views and opinions have been shared practitioners can invite parents to work with them on the resolution, 'It has been really useful to talk about the problem Joe has had. Do you have any ideas about how best to help him deal with it?'

◆ **Thank the parent**. Finally, when it is likely a shared solution has been identified; thank the parent for sharing their concerns and working with you to help resolve the situation. A shared solution may be identified immediately or need some more time and a further meeting. Either is fine. The key issue is to ensure that a shared solution is found.

Supporting families during life transitions

During the course of early education, children and families can experience transitions in their life, including divorce, illness, bereavement, employment and house moves (Braun, 2001). For young children, the impact of these can be significant and it may take time for them to adjust. For example, after divorce children may see significantly less of one parent, illness may reduce levels of contact between a parent and child, or a house move may disrupt contact with other members of the family and friends. These changes also bring with them a need for parents to adjust. This may be associated with changes in parenting, possibly being less sensitive to the needs of children or increased levels of conflict within the family (Woollett, 1999).

In many respects, practitioners cannot influence these events directly but can be an invaluable source of support for the family. Ensuring that there is time for family members to talk, maintaining a positive and non-judgemental approach, and providing a warm and supportive environment for the child in the setting will help the family to face the situation more confidently. In some cases it may be appropriate to direct families towards other services to receive guidance and support, and this should be considered. When families are experiencing difficult situations they are likely to be grateful to know that there are additional services available that can support them.

Levels of involvement

Within early years settings it is not unusual, for a variety of reasons, to have some parents who require a significant amount of support in terms of time. This may occur due to apprehension about transition into or out of the setting, or may be linked to the parent situation or home environment. Other concerns centre on child safety, security, happiness and well-being (Evans, 2002). Whatever the reason, the aim for practitioners is to have a non-judgemental approach, avoid criticism and aim to see the parent's perspective. At times it may be tempting to ask parents if there is something going on at home. Even if there is an issue, however, a parent may feel this is private and, in many respects, would knowing make a difference to the response? Irrespective of the response, practitioners should be supportive, empathetic and gentle (Gonzalez-Mena and Stonehouse, 2000). An alternative approach is to let parents know that they can talk to you, which is likely to lead to a more trusting and, ultimately, open relationship and one where the parent feels comfortable. Gonzalez-Mena and Stonehouse (2000) and Evans (2002) offer the following practical advice for developing partnership working with parents:

- Involve parents in decision-making, possibly approaching them first to ask their opinion. Communication is the key to success.

- Encourage parents to bring their concerns to you and agree a time to meet and give feedback on the issue they have raised.

- Respond flexibly and supportively to each situation.

- Make parents feel valued.

- Think about what parents want for their child and make clear goals to support this.

- Be prepared to negotiate and compromize.

- Ask parents openly if they feel the setting is meeting their child's needs and allow parents to offer their perspective without feeling defensive.

- Focus on communicating good news and be selective about giving bad news. This does not mean avoiding discussion of difficult issues but ensuring there is a specific focus, e.g. aim to develop sharing in play sessions.

- Be aware of the boundaries of your own experience – do you need support from a colleague or another agency?

- Reflect on situations and learn from them.

Comments are made between practitioners about the home environment of particular children, which can be associated with the idea that some parents, such as poor and ethnic minority families, do not value or provide for their child. For the vast majority of parents this is inaccurate as they have a deep concern about their child's achievements. Many families may have changes in their life that present particular challenges to them, including location moves or changes in family structure. For families with adversities, early years setting may be seen as a stable and safe environment for their child, a place where children are safe and secure. When children are at the setting parents may feel that this is the only occasion that they are able to attend to other concerns (Lawson, 2003).

Hilliard *et al.* (2001) describe how some practitioners talk of 'waiting years' for parents to start doing things to support the setting. For example, reading with their child or asking questions to promote understanding and learning. In comparison, Lawson (2003) found that parents were eager to share their stories but only did so when asked and saw involvement as starting in the community and moving into the setting. In the same study, some parents identified a perceived lack of affection towards children from practitioners and described situations where they felt their children were seen as objects waiting to be taught. This emphasizes the importance of social and emotional warmth in interactions with each family.

For some parents, their experiences of education may have been extremely negative, so, unsurprisingly, they are likely to be wary of becoming involved through fear of exposing themselves to similar situations. Added to this is the fact that the majority of interactions occur on *setting turf*, where family members are likely to feel much less secure. To overcome this, practitioners need to work at building a trusting relationship, where parents trust practitioners and practitioners trust parents. To have an effective partnership, it is important for practitioners to understand the history, needs and barriers to involvement that each individual family may present. From this, approaches that support and value families as opposed to exclude and stigmatize can be planned. To achieve this, the relationship needs to empower parents and give them confidence in their parenting role, with the aim of avoiding or removing the idea of expert (the practitioner) versus novice (the parent) (File, 2001). To achieve this, important issues for practitioners to address are:

♦ Do all parents have equal access to all aspects of the environment.

♦ Are requests for help directed to all groups of parents (not a minority who are always involved)?

♦ Is there recognition that the role of parent is different from that of the practitioner?

If practitioners can show awareness of the needs of individual families as well as the setting, the roles of practitioner and parent are more likely to be complimentary and will contribute to children achieving their potential (Todd and Higgins, 1998).

This section has provided an overview of a number

of areas where barriers may impede parental involvement, but is not meant to be interpreted as
suggesting that these are the only areas where
difficulties can occur. It does aim to highlight that
these issues have been identified as leading to
barriers and a breakdown in parent partnerships. In
many respects, the objective of overcoming barriers
should be more about ensuring inclusive services that
see difference as a benefit not a deficit.

6

Evaluation and Self-reflection

Parental partnerships: identifying the next steps

When change has been implemented, evaluation can identify what has worked well, what may need amending and the direction for continued development. Evaluation can be useful after alterations to practice or the learning environment or when new strategies have been implemented to develop partnership between the setting, families and community. Research evidence and guidance from organisations that aim to promote partnership between settings, the home and wider community can assist practitioners in the process of evaluation.

Eldridge (2001) makes links between family partnership and the policies within the setting. This provides a useful starting point for guiding developments to establish effective partnerships with each family. To lower any potential barriers to partnership, the learning environment and approaches of the practitioners need to be open and accepting. To guide practitioners in this, Eldridge suggests a number of questions that they should ask themselves to check their progress:

♦ Are families welcomed as partners in their children's schooling?

Parent Partnership in the Early Years

- Is communication clear and accessible to each family?

- Is each parent involved in his or her child's learning?

- Does parent literature include clear information about how and why the help from parents is needed?

- Does the organization allow for a variety of times and ways for families to participate?

- Is anybody excluded for any reason?

Moyles *et al.* (2002) have produced a framework for use by practitioners to support self-reflection on what contributes to effective practice in early years. They list a number of questions that practitioners can use to reflect on aspects of practice (p. 51). To what degree did the approach or activity:

- Establish respectful relationships with parents that are reciprocal and collaborative?

- Build parents' trust and confidence and enable two-way exchange of information?

- Show recognition, respect and equality of opportunity with consideration for ethnicity, culture, religion, home language and family background?

- Have knowledge and understanding of how to help parents understand early education processes and content through direct knowledge of family and community background?

Early years curriculum documents also set out

expectations and provide guidance on why family partnership is vital and how it can be achieved. The significance of this is emphasized in the Curriculum Guidance for England through stating that this is a central requirement for effective teaching, a point supported by Moyles *et al.* (2002).

Within the New Zealand early years curriculum Te Whariki, which covers the education and care of children from birth to school entry, there are a number of reflective questions (Ministry of Education, 1996). These are linked to goals within the curriculum and are designed as a basis for further discussion. This approach can help to link the actual curriculum, including partnerships with families, with the process of evaluation, as detailed below:

- In what way are staff able to be a resource for parents and families? Can this be done in any other ways?

- How is daily information about children shared with parents or family and between adults who work with the children? How well does this meet the needs?

- How is knowledge about children collected and shared among adults who work with them, and does this provide sufficient information for those who need it?

- How do adults find out and make use of children's favourite stories, songs and rhymes?

- How are parents involved in the child management and guidance polices of the setting?

Parent Partnership in the Early Years

- To what extent do adults include phrases from children's home languages when talking with them?

- How is the use of community language incorporated into the programme, such as at story time?

These questions, as well as guiding the development of practice, may assist in an informal evaluation of a new approach to partnership at an early stage of implementation to guide minor changes. For example, after a new approach to parent conferences with an initial group of parents it could be decided that more opportunities are needed to enable parents to be actively involved in decisions affecting their children. The following stories show how two

---

Story A

During a recent meeting between a group of parents and the key worker, there had been a long conversation about the importance of play for children. Many parents had commented though that it can be costly to provide appropriate toys for children, especially as they need to be replaced. The key worker agreed and asked parents if they felt the setting could do anything to help. The group decided to talk this over with other parents. After a couple of weeks parents approached the setting with the idea of setting up a toy library. To assist parents the setting made a display area available to parents to publicize the idea, gave a questionnaire to each parent to collect their views on the proposed development and provided a suggestion box to collect feedback from all parents.

Story B

The staff team at Treetops nursery have decided that
they want to redesign the information pack given to
each family prior to their child starting at the setting. The
aim of the exercise was to ensure that the pack is
relevant to all families and addresses the issues that are
important to them. To achieve this it was decided that a
formal evaluation process was appropriate. A feedback
form was designed and sent to each parent with a letter
explaining the reasons for collecting their views. Once
the feedback was collected a notice asking parents to
form an advisory group was displayed and informal
approaches were made to parents in the setting. This
attracted nine parents who represented the diversity of
families within the setting. A meeting was arranged and
parents were asked for further information about the
areas identified for development in the feedback forms.
During a further two meetings parents were shown
examples of the redesigned materials and further
alterations were made based on their feedback. Informal
discussions with new parents suggested that the
information was well received.

---

different early years settings carried out evaluation. In
the first example the setting responded to a
conversation. Parents managed the majority of the
evaluation with minimal support from the setting. The
second example deals a more formal approach and
clearly shows how input from parents is a key factor
in ensuring that the new information is relevant.

These two examples show that the method of
evaluation needs to suit the aims. To achieve this,

decisions have to be made on the mechanism that is most suitable for the specific activity. It is likely that this decision will be influenced by the aims of the evaluation. Informal strategies, such as conversation at the beginning or end of the day or feedback on an information display, can be useful for gaining opinion on new ideas, as in Story A. For more formal activities, particularly when it involves changes in practice or procedures more formal methods of evaluation can be utilized, as in Story B. These can include forms requesting feedback on an aspect of service, completing scales to rate the content of a workshop or a survey of all parents to guide a major development, such as new premises.

The suggestions in this section do not cover every area of evaluation but provide a starting point and offer guidance about the areas to consider and the questions that could be asked. Finally, one of the most important messages to communicate to those offering feedback is that their comments are valued and will be used to inform future practice (Edwards and Warin, 1999).

Conclusion

There are clearly many challenges for early years settings in establishing effective partnerships with parents. Hall *et al.* (2001) state that the aim is:

... to establish a community of learners who think reflectively and who collaborate in the construction of knowledge. We believe that the collective combinations of children, families and teachers are vital to our learning community' (p. 53)

There are clear benefits of partnership working for families, practitioners and the wider community, not least in terms of child achievement and educational outcomes. There are also opportunities for the development of current practice, for example, when working with fathers. To establish and maintain effective partnerships practitioners will need to invest time and effort. This may be in terms of acquiring skills, developing their practice and exploring new ways of working as a team. To make this task manageable, settings will need to evaluate their practice and identify any relevant issues, such as the amount of administration support available to practitioners (Eldridge, 2001). It is also clear, though, that practitioners do not need to take responsibility for all aspects of partnership. Arguably, the potential for the best approaches to partnership will come when there is full participation and involvement of all partners.

Practitioners need to remain aware of the central needs of each child and, at the same time, have realistic expectations of parents. To develop effective partnerships, the starting point needs to be linked to the current position of parents and move forward in an enabling manner. To achieve this, it is vital to establish trust, show respect, provide encouragement and maintain two-way communication. There are clearly challenges in this, but a collaborative approach will benefit children both today and far into the future.

References

Adams, K.S. and Christenson, S.L. (2000) 'Trust and family-school relationship. Examination of parent-teacher differences in elementary and secondary grades', *Journal of School Psychology*, Vol. 38, No. 5, pp. 477–97.

Ainsworth, M.D.S., Blehar, M.C., Walters, E. and Wall, S. (1978) *Patterns of Attachment*, New Jersey: Lawrence Erlbaum.

Anderson, H., Adlam, T., Coltman, P., Cotton, E. and Daniels, R. (2002) 'Spinning the plates: organising the early years classroom', in D. Whitebread (ed.) *Teaching and Learning in the Early Years*, London: Routledge Farmer, pp. 23–54.

Bailey, D.B. (2001) 'Evaluating parental involvement and family support in early intervention and preschool programs', *Journal of Early Intervention*, Vol. 24, No. 1, pp. 1–14.

Basic Skills Agency (2003) *'National Support Project for Storysacks'*, BSA, available at http://www.basic-skills.co.uk/ [last accessed 26/05/03].

Bergman, H. and Hobson, B. (2002) 'Compulsory fatherhood: the coding of fatherhood in the Swedish welfare state', in B. Hobson (ed.) *Making Men into Fathers: Men, Masculinities and the Social Politics of Fatherhood*, Cambridge University Press, pp. 92–124.

Braun, D. (2001) 'Perspective on parenting', In P. Foley, J. Roche, and S. Tucker (eds) *Children in Society: Contemporary Theory, Policy and Practice*, Hampshire: Palgrave, pp. 239–248.

Bruce, T. (1997) *Early Childhood Education* (2nd edition), London: Hodder and Stoughton.

Bruce, T. and Meggitt, C. (2002) *Child Care and education* (3rd edition), London: Hodder and Stoughton.

Caplan, J., Hall, G., Lubin, S. and Fleming, R. (1997) 'Literature Review of School-Family Partnerships', North Carolina Regional Educational Laboratory, available at http://www.ncrel.org/sdrs/pidata/pi01trev.htm [last accessed 30/03/03].

Casper, V. and Schultz, S. B. (1999) *Gay Parents/Straight Schools: Building Communication and Trust*, New York: Teachers College Press.

Chaboudy, R., Jameson, R. and Huber, P. (2001) 'Connecting families and schools through technology', *Book Report*, Vol. 20, No. 2, pp. 52-7.

Coates, J. (2003) *Men Talk*, Oxford: Blackwell.

Curtis, A. (1998) *A Curriculum for the Preschool Child* (2nd Edition), London: Routledge.

Dahlberg, G., Moss, P. and Pence, A. (1999) *Beyond Quality in Early Childhood, Education and Care*, London: Falmer Press.

Dalli, C. (2002) 'From home to childcare: challenges for mothers, teachers and children', in H. Fabian and A. Dunlop (eds), *Transitions in the Early Years: Debating Continuity and Progression for Young Children in Early Education*, London: Routledge Farmer, pp. 38-51.

Daniels, H. (1996) 'The best practice project: building', *Educational Leadership*, Vol. 53, No. 7, pp. 38-43.

Daper, L. and Duffy, B. (2001) 'Working with parents', in G. Pugh (ed.) *Contemporary Issues in the Early Years: Working Collaboratively for Children*, London: Paul Chapman Publishing.

Edwards, A. and Knight, P. (1997) 'Parents and professionals', in B. Cosin and M. Hales (eds.) *Families, Education and Social Differences*, London: Routledge.

Edwards, A. and Warin, J. (1999) 'Parental involvement in raising the achievement of primary school pupils: why bother?' *Oxford Review of Education*, Vol. 25, No. 3, pp. 325–41.

Eldridge, D. (2001) 'Parental Involvement: It's Worth the Effort', *Young Children*, Vol. 56, No. 4, pp. 65–69.

Epstein, J. L. and Saunders, M. G. (2002) 'Family, school and community partnerships', in M. H. Bornstein (ed.) *Handbook of Parenting Volume 5: Practical Issues in Parenting* (2nd edition), London: Lawrence Erlbaum Associates.

Equal Opportunities Commission (2002) *Men and Women; Who Looks After the Children? report on Three Joint Seminars*, EOC.

Equal Opportunities Commission (2003) *Fathers: Balancing Work and Family*, EOC.

Evans, M. (2002) 'Not to Worry', *Nursery world*, pp. 22–3.

Featherstone, B. (2003) 'Taking Fathers Seriously', *British Journal of Social Work*, Vol. 33, pp. 239–54.

File, N. (2001) 'Family professional partnerships: practice that matches philosophy', *Young Children*, Vol. 56, No. 4, pp. 70–4.

Flouri, E. and Buchanan, A. (2003) 'What predicts fathers' involvement with their children? A prospective study of intact families', *British Journal of Developmental Psychology*, Vol. 21, No. 1, 81–9.

Foot, H., Howe, C., Cheyne, B., Terras, M. and Rattray, C. (2000) 'Pre-school education: parents' preferences, knowledge and expectations', *International Journal of Early Years Education*, Vol. 8, No. 3, pp. 189–204.

Forman, G. and Fyfe, B. (1998) 'Negotiated learning through design, documentation and discourse', in C. Edwards, L. Gandini and G. Forman (eds.), *The Hundred Languages of Children* (2nd edition), London: Ablex Publishing Corporation, pp. 239–60.

Parent Partnership in the Early Years

Frieman, B. B. and Berkeley, T. R. (2002) 'Encouraging fathers to participate in the school experiences of young children: the teacher's role', *Early Childhood Education Journal*, Vol. 29, No. 3, pp. 209–13.

Gandini, L. (1998) 'Educational and caring spaces', in C. Edwards, L. Gandini and G. Forman (eds.), *The Hundred Languages of Children* (2nd edition), London: Ablex Publishing Corporation, pp. 161–78.

Gonzalez-Mena, J. and Stonehouse, A. (2000) 'High-maintenance parents', *Childcare Information Exchange*, No. 131, pp. 10–12.

Greenman, J. (2001) 'Empowering parents', *Childcare Information Exchange*, No. 138, pp. 56–9.

Griebel, W. and Niesel, R. (2002) 'Co-constructing transition into kindergarten and school by children, parents and teachers', in H. Fabian and A. Dunlop (eds), *Transitions in the Early Years: Debating Continuity and Progression for Young Children in Early Education*, London: Routledge Farmer, pp. 64–75.

Hadow report (1931) *The Primary School*, Board of Education, HMSO.

Hall, E., Oleson, V. and Gambetti, A. (2001) 'Including parents in the process of documentation', *Childcare Information Exchange*, No. 138, pp. 52–5.

Hartup, W. W. (1998) 'The company they keep: friendships and their developmental significance', in A. Campbell and S. Muncer (eds.), *The Social Child*, Hove: Psychology Press, pp.143–64.

Hearn, J. (2002) 'Men, fathers and the state', in B. Hobson (ed.) *Making Men into Fathers: Men, Masculinities and the Social Politics of Fatherhood*, Cambridge University Press, pp. 125–49.

Hilliard, D., Pelo, A. and Carter, M. (2001) 'Changing out attitude and actions in working with families', *Childcare Information Exchange*, Vol. 138, pp. 48–51.

Jaffee, S. R., Moffitt, T. E., Caspi, A. and Taylor, A. (2003)

'Life with (or without) father: the benefits of living with two biological parents depends on the father's antisocial behaviour', *Child Development*, Vol. 74, No. 1, pp. 109–26.

Jordan, L., Reyes-Blanes, M. E., Peel, B. B., Peel, H. A. and Lane, H. B. (1998) 'Developing teacher–parent partnerships across cultures: effective parent conferences', *Intervention in School and Clinic*, Vol. 33, No. 3, pp. 141–7.

Keyes, C. (2002) 'A way of thinking about parent/teacher partnership for teachers', *Journal of Early Years Education*, Vol. 10, No. 3, pp. 177–91.

Keyser, J. (2001) 'Creating partnerships with families: problem-solving through communication', *Childcare Information Exchange*, No. 138, pp. 44–7.

Knijn, T. and Selten, P. (2002) 'Transformations of fatherhood: the Netherlands', in B. Hobson (ed.) *Making Men into Fathers: Men, Masculinities and the Social Politics of Fatherhood*, Cambridge University Press, pp. 168–90.

Kraft-Sayre, M. E. and Pianta, R. C. (2000) *Enhancing the Transition to Kindergarten*, Charlottesville: University of West Virginia, National Centre for Early Development and Learning.

Lawson, M. A. (2003) 'School-family relations in context. Parent and teacher perceptions of parental involvement', *Urban Education*, Vol. 38, No. 1, pp. 77–133.

Levine, J. A. (1993) 'Involving fathers in Head Start: A framework for public policy and programme development', *Families in Society*, Vol. 74, pp. 4–19.

Lewis, J. (2002) 'The Problem of fathers; policy and behaviour in Britain', in B. Hobson (ed.) *Making Men into Fathers: Men, Masculinities and the Social Politics of Fatherhood*, Cambridge University Press, pp. 125–49.

Long, M. (2000) *The Psychology of Education*, London: Routledge Farmer.

Macleod, F. (2000) 'Low attendance by fathers at family

literacy events: Some tentative explanations', *Early Childhood Development and Care,* Vol. 161, pp. 107–19.

Malaguzzi, L. (1998) 'History, ideas and basic philosophy: an interview with Lella Gandini', in C. Edwards, L. Gandini and G. Forman (eds.), *The Hundred Languages of Children* (2nd edition), London: Ablex Publishing Corporation, pp. 49–98.

Mayo, M. (1998) 'The shifting concept of community', in M. Allott, and M. Robb (eds), *Understanding Health and Social Care: An Introductory Reader,* London: Sage/Open University, pp. 104–110.

McBride, B. A., Rane, T. R. and Bae, J. (2001) 'Intervening with teachers to encourage father/male involvement in early childhood programs', *Early Childhood Research Quarterly,* Vol. 16, No. 1, 77–93.

McWilliam, R. A., Tocci, L. and Harbin, G. L. (1998) 'Family-centered services: service providers' discourse and behaviour', *Topics in Early Childhood Special Education,* Vol. 18, No. 4, pp. 206–22.

Ministry of Education (1996) *Te Whariki: Early Childhood Curriculum,* New Zealand: Learning Media Limited.

Moyles, J, Adams, S. and Musgrove, A. (2002) *SPEEL: Study of Pedagogical Effectiveness in Early Learning,* Anglia Polytechnic University and Department for Education and Skills, London: HMSO.

National Centre for Early Development and Learning (1999) *Education in the Early Years: A Conference for States on Early Childhood Education,* NCEDL/United states Department of Education, available at http://www.fpg.unc.edu/~ncedl/PDFs/ed_early_years.pdf [last accessed 30/03/03].

National Children's Bureau (2000) *Integration in Practice: The Report of a National Study to Identify Common Areas of Quality in Early Years and Childcare,* National Children's Bureau on behalf of the Department for

Education and Employment.

Neuman, M. (2002) 'The wider context: an international overview of transition issues', in H. Fabian and A. Dunlop (eds.), *Transitions in the Early Years: Debating Continuity and Progression for Young Children in Early Education*, London: Routledge Farmer, pp. 8–22.

Parentline Plus (2003) *Helping Children Learn: Pre-school Children Information Sheet 1*, Parentline Plus, available at www.parentlineplus.org.uk/data/publications/index.html [last accessed 28/05/2003].

Parker, C. (2002) 'Working with families on the curriculum: developing shared understanding of children's mark making', in C. Nutbrown (ed.) *Research Studies in Early Childhood Education*, Stoke-on-Trent, Trentham.

Patterson, C. J. and Redding, R. E. (1996) 'Lesbian and Gay families with children: Implications of social science research for policy'. *Journal of Social Issues*, Vol. 52, No. 3, pp. 29–50.

Perry, B. and Dockett, S. (2003) *Starting School: Perspectives of Australian Children, Parents and Educators. Proceedings of the British Educational Research Association conference*, Edinburgh, September 11–13.

Pleck, J. H. (1997) 'Parental involvement: levels sources and consequences' in M. E. Lamb (ed.), *The Role of the father in Child Development* (3rd edition), New York: Wiley, pp. 61–103.

Plowden Report (1967) *Children and their Primary Schools*, Central Advisory Council for Education, London: HMSO.

Pryor, J. and Rodgers, B. (2001) *Children in Changing Families: Life After Parental Separation*, Oxford: Blackwell.

Pugh, G. (2001) 'A policy for early childhood services', in Pugh, G. (ed.) *Contemporary Issues in the Early Years* (3rd edition), London: Paul Chapman.

Qualification and Curriculum Authority (2002) *Building the*

Foundation Stage Profile: Training Materials for the Foundation Stage Video, London: QCA.

Qualification and Curriculum Authority and Department for Education and Employment (2000) *Investing in Our Future: Curriculum Guidance for the Foundation Stage*, London: QCA/DfEE.

Roberts, M. (2001) 'Childcare policy', in P. Foley, J. Roche and S. Tucker (eds.) *Children in Society: Contemporary Theory, Policy and Practice*, Hampshire: Palgrave, pp. 52–64.

Roberts, R. (2002) *Self-esteem and Early Learning* (2nd edition), London: Paul Chapman.

Roggman, L. A., Boyce, L. K., Cook, G. A. and Jump, V. K. (2001) 'Inside home visits: a collaborative look at process and quality', *Early Childhood Research Quarterly*, Vol. 16, pp. 53–71.

Rolfe, H., Metcalfe, H., Anderson, T. and Meadows, P. (2003) *Recruitment and Retention of Childcare, Early Years and Play Workers: Research Study*, National Institute of Economic and Social Research and Department for Education and Skills, London: HMSO.

Rosenkoetter, S. E. (2001) 'Come for a bedtime story', *Young Children*, Vol. 56, No. 3, pp. 86–7.

Schaffer, H. R. (1998) *Social Development*, Oxford: Blackwell.

Smidt, S. (2002) *A Guide to Early Years Practice* (2nd edition), London: Routledge Farmer.

Smith, P. K., Cowie, H. and Blades, M. (2003) *Understanding Children's Development*, Oxford: Blackwell.

Steedman, C. (1990) *Childhood, Culture and Class in Britain: Margaret McMillan 1860–1931*, London: Virago Press Limited.

Storkey, E. (1991) 'Race, ethnicity and gender', in *D103: Society and Social Science*, Milton Keynes: Open University.

Sure Start (2000) *Providing Good Quality Childcare and*

Early Learning Experiences through Sure Start, London: DfEE.

Sumison, J. (2000) 'Negotiating otherness: a male early childhood educator's gender positioning', *International Journal of Early Years Education*, Vol. 8, No. 2, pp. 129–40.

Sylva, K, Melhuish, E., Siraj-Blatchford, I, Taggart, B. and Elliot, K. (2003) *The Effective Provision of Pre-School Education (EPPE) Project: Findings from the Pre-school Period*, Institute of Education/DfES, available at http://www.ioe.ac.uk/cdl/eppe/pdfs/eppe_brief2503.pdf [last accessed 10/05/03].

Thompson, N. (2001) *Anti-Discriminatory Practice* (3rd edition), Hampshire: Palgrave.

Tizard, B. and Hughes, M. (2002) *Young Children Learning* (2nd edition), Oxford: Blackwell Publishing.

Todd, E. S. and Higgins, S. (1998) 'Powerlessness in professional and parent partnerships', *British Journal of Sociology of Education*, Vol. 19, No. 2, pp. 227–36.

Trowell, J. (2002) 'Setting the scene', in J. Trowell and A. Etchegoyen (eds.) *The Importance of Fathers: A Psychoanalytic Re-evaluation*, East Sussex: Bruner-Routledge, pp. 3–19.

Turbiville, V. P., Umbarger, G. T. and Guthrie, A. (2000) 'Father's involvement in programs for young children', *Young Children*, Vol. 55, No. 4, pp. 74–9.

United States Department of Education (2002) *Teaching Our Youngest: A Guide for Preschool Teachers and Child Care and Family Providers*, United States Department of Education, available at *http://www.ed.gov/offices/OESE/teachingouryoungest/communicate.html* [last accessed 30/03/2003].

Whalley, M. (2001) *Involving Parents in their Children's Learning*, London: Paul Chapman.

Woollett, A. (1999) 'Families and their role in children's

lives and development', in Messer, D. and Millar, S. (eds.) *Exploring Developmental Psychology*, London: Arnold.